HOW TO COOK A HIPPOPOTAMUS

How to Cook a
HIPPOPOTAMUS

THE FOLIO BOOK OF
QUAINT AND CURIOUS ADVICE

BEING A BRIEF ANTHOLOGY OF *DUBIOUS*
AND *DANGEROUS* INFORMATION

*Containing Much FANCIFUL INSTRUCTION
on How to Choose a Wife, How to Avoid Work, How
to Smile and Amuse Children; as well as Guidance
on Roughing It, Cultivating a Magnetic Gaze,
Defending Yourself against a Mad Dog and on
How to Visit an Old English Inn; to which
is Added a Hangman's Ready Reckoner
and Certain Other Items of Interest*

ALL VERY PROPER TO BE READ
AND KEPT IN EVERY FAMILY

selected by IAN PINDAR
and illustrated by JOHN HOLDER

'*Credo quia absurdum est*'

PRINTED FOR MEMBERS OF
THE FOLIO SOCIETY
44 EAGLE STREET LONDON MMVI

First published by The Folio Society Ltd 2006

Selection and editorial matter © Ian Pindar 2006

The right of Ian Pindar to be identified as the editor of this
Work has been asserted by him in accordance with the
Copyright, Designs and Patents Act 1988.

Illustrations © John Holder 2006

TYPESET IN NEW CENTURY SCHOOLBOOK
AT THE FOLIO SOCIETY. PRINTED BY BATH PRESS
COLOURBOOKS, GLASGOW, AND BOUND
AT THE BATH PRESS, BATH

Contents

The Preface to the Reader ix

Excellent Remedies for Various Ailments 1

↦ *To Cure the Toothache 1* ↦ *Avoiding Bites and Stings 1* ↦ *Two Cures for Baldness 2* ↦ *Arsenic Cures 2* ↦ *To Stop Bleeding 3* ↦ *A Word about Gout 5* ↦ *The Medicinal Qualities of Tobacco 6* ↦ *A Universal Remedy 7* ↦ *The Wonders of the Air-Bath 7* ↦ *A Painless Method for Curing Piles 8* ↦ *A Remedy for Melancholy 10* ↦ *Cures for Whooping Cough 11* ↦ *The Proper Use of the Warm Bath 11* ↦ *How to Cure a Madman 11* ↦ *The Alcoholic Cured 12* ↦ *A Remedy for Sleeplessness 12* ↦ *The Importance of Fresh Air 12*

Essential Etiquette 14

↦ *The Market Value of Good Manners 14* ↦ *The Importance of Conformity 15* ↦ *How to Converse in Society 16* ↦ *Onions, etc. 17* ↦ *When to Make an Introduction 17* ↦ *How to Converse with Ladies 18* ↦ *Pulling out One's Watch 19* ↦ *A Word on Posture and Bearing 19* ↦ *The Correct Arrangement of the Male Organs 20* ↦ *Gloves 20* ↦ *Stairs 20* ↦ *On the Street 21* ↦ *How to Host a Dinner Party 22* ↦ *How to Eat 23*

Delicious Recipes for Discerning Chefs 24

↦ *Sugar Mice 24* ↦ *A Hunter's Breakfast 24* ↦ *Turtle Soup 26* ↦ *Raw Meat Juice 26* ↦ *Brain Fritters 27* ↦ *Roast Tongue and Udder 27* ↦ *Bear Rump Roast 27* ↦ *How to Cook a Hippopotamus 28* ↦ *Seventeen Squirrels in a Pot 29* ↦ *Crunchy Frogs 29* ↦ *How to Cook and Eat a Live Goose 30*

Flawless Beauty Tips for Plain People 32

↦ *How to Stay Young 32* ↦ *Bathing Beauties 33* ↦ *Washing the Hair 33* ↦ *To Remove Freckles 34* ↦ *Banishing Black Spots 34* ↦ *A Word of Advice Regarding Corsets 35* ↦ *Removing Tartar 37* ↦ *How to Stop Blushing 38* ↦ *For Tired Eyes 38* ↦ *A Word about Chins 38*

ADVICE OF A DELICATE NATURE 40

⁎ *Continence 40* ⁎ *Concerning 'Strange Women' 41* ⁎ *How to Choose a Wife 42* ⁎ *A Note about 'Popping' the Question 44* ⁎ *How to Spoil a Husband 44* ⁎ *Building up Your Wife's Breasts 46*

SOME EXCELLENT OBSERVATIONS ON THE DUTIES OF PARENTHOOD 47

⁎ *Fitness for Parenthood 47* ⁎ *Preparing for Parenthood 47* ⁎ *How to Improve the Race 48* ⁎ *Success with Suckling 51* ⁎ *Cold Baths are Best 51* ⁎ *A Note on Tobacco and Children 51* ⁎ *To Prevent an Outburst of Spirits 52* ⁎ *How to Amuse Children 52* ⁎ *Trussed Fowls 52* ⁎ *Impressions with Sealing Wax 53* ⁎ *Cards in a Hat 53* ⁎ *Wayside Cribbage 53* ⁎ *Family Coach 54* ⁎ *Dolls 54* ⁎ *Games: A Word of Caution 55*

WISE WORDS FOR EXPLORERS AND EXCURSIONISTS ALIKE 56

⁎ *A French Revolution in Fast Food 56* ⁎ *How to Visit an Old English Inn 57* ⁎ *How to Become a Blood-Brother 58* ⁎ *How to Rough It 59* ⁎ *How to Become an Alpinist 60* ⁎ *How to Speak Arabic 63* ⁎ *Native Pipe-Smoking 63* ⁎ *Rules for Motorists 65* ⁎ *Motor Hooliganism 65* ⁎ *How to Behave on a Sinking Ship 66*

INTRODUCING THE OCCULT TO THE CURIOUS 68

⁎ *Automatic Writing for Beginners 68* ⁎ *Ghosts in Photographs 68* ⁎ *How to Cultivate a Magnetic Gaze 70* ⁎ *How to Read a Crystal Ball 71* ⁎ *How to be a Clairvoyante 73* ⁎ *Familiar Spirits 74* ⁎ *A Summary of Your Mental Powers 76*

IN TIME OF WAR 77

⁎ *Handling Self-Abuse in Wartime 77* ⁎ *How to Stalk Your Neighbour 78* ⁎ *How to Put a Bomb in a Post Office 79* ⁎ *French for the Front 81*

LIFE SKILLS GUARANTEED TO FETCH OUT THE
CAPACITIES AND ABILITIES OF PERSONS OF QUALITY 83

↝ *How to be Amused 83* ↝ *How to Smile 84* ↝ *How to Shoot a Giraffe 86* ↝ *Improving Your Memory 87* ↝ *How to Cultivate the Body 87* ↝ *How to Smoke 88* ↝ *How to Perform an Emergency Baptism 89* ↝ *How to Defend Yourself against a Mad Dog 90* ↝ *On Hanging Considered as One of the Fine Arts 90* ↝ *The Perfect Public Hanging 92* ↝ *A Ready Reckoner for Hangmen 94* ↝ *Hints for Hiring Servants in the Colonies 95* ↝ *How to Take a Strong Man Prisoner Single-Handed 96* ↝ *How to Execute a Legitimate 'Rabbit-Killer' Punch 97* ↝ *How to Treat a Hysteric 98* ↝ *How to Stop a Runaway Horse 98* ↝ *How to Tell an Imbecile from an Idiot 98* ↝ *Suicide for Scouts 99* ↝ *How to be a Ventriloquist 100* ↝ *How to Seize Control of the Means of Production 102* ↝ *How to Avoid Work 103*

SOURCES 105

ACKNOWLEDGEMENTS 110

INDEX 111

To
ISABELLE

ut incunabula tibi emere possim

THE PREFACE TO THE READER

by the Late Montgomery 'Bunty' Burrows

author of
A Few Words to Schoolmistresses, Too Much Pork for a Shilling
and *The Utilisation of Street Dust*

OPPORTUNITIES ARE RARE for an author of advanced years to exercise his faculties upon the general public, so imagine my delight and surprise when the editor of this informative volume, no doubt exhausted from his labours, invited me to compose a few words on the important subject of advice, an enthusiasm that has not lessened with the discovery that I will receive but small payment for the pleasure.

It is well said that there is nothing we receive with so much reluctance as advice. And yet, when the rush of the day's work is over, in the cool of the evening, when the children are all safely in bed and when you have a chance of a quiet half-hour with no work to do, then is the time you will appreciate this little gem of a book.

The research, the accuracy, the precision this work demanded are quite unprecedented and it is no discredit to the editor that he lacked these qualities. The Reader will observe that almost the entire volume consists of fragments from old books, albeit subjected to the very latest scrutiny. I am told they have been lightly edited to conform to modern standards of 'readability', a word I abhor, but to go into minute detail on the subject would only try the patience of the Reader. Some of the advice offered here will appear ill-conceived and even a little dangerous to more sceptical natures, but it is my firm belief that this treasury of ancient wisdom will become a standard work of reference for many centuries to come and will prove of infinite service to all mankind.

There is not a man jack or woman jill among you who will not benefit from a close inspection of its pages, particularly if you are an invalid or a person of lax moral fibre and weak digestion. How to converse in society, improve your memory, visit an Old English inn, stop a runaway horse and cook a hippopotamus are secrets well worth knowing. As is the correct arrangement of the male organs.

A cynical philosopher has said we are all madmen, with lucid intervals of longer or shorter duration. I must have recently come to the end of a lucid interval, for a few days ago I sought the advice of a mortal enemy of mine from whom I have suffered endless insults over the years. My solicitor has advised me to refer to this odious medical man simply as Dr X.

I do not mind telling you, Dear Reader, that lately I have been overtaken by a malady of an extremely delicate and worrying nature, namely a total suppression of urine. Knowing this disorder to be in almost all instances deadly, I was moved in my distress to update my will and put my papers in order. I was also unwise enough to invite to my bedside the aforementioned Dr X and to confide in this insufferable rogue my trouble.

I am sad to say that his worst nature was provoked by my predicament, for all the advice he could give me was this: 'Well, Bunty Burrows,' he said, 'if you cannot make water you had better make earth!'

Reader, doubt it not, I have only myself to blame, but I have hope and, thanks to Mr Pindar, an opportunity this instant to make of my own sad case an example to all. Allow me now to impart to you some advice drawn from my own sorry experience.

When Lord Bacon affirms that 'strength of nature passes over many excesses which are owing a man until he is old' I am ashamed to say that he is stating the very facts of my own situation. Nature grants us these indulgences gratis at the beginning, but at the end she sends in her account. These sins of youth have not only destroyed my health but have sullied my manhood, tainting, as well as impairing, my whole nature, rising up in my final years to scourge me.

Believe it, Dear Reader, there is a reckoning time in this mortal life apart from any that awaits us in the world to come. There is a judgement day in the nerves and bones and heart and brain! Oh the deep damnation there is in secret sins, which the physician neither sees nor probes nor cauterises nor, alas, cures.

I do not believe there is anyone who is trying to live aright who ever looked on any lustful picture or lascivious sight who will not acknowledge that once to have seen it is to remember it as though it were branded in the brain; or whoever heard a salacious song or suggestive story, where wickedness was sheathed in wit, who does not regret and to his dying day will not have cause to regret such things.

Speaking for myself, I can only say that there are things I learned when I was a lad, there are songs and stories I listened to and laughed at sixty years ago or more which have left their poison in my mind and heart—and I tell you today that if any surgeon's knife were LONG enough and SHARP enough to cut the SINFUL cancerous roots clean out of my memory, I would submit to the operation on the spot!

I am being pressed to lie down by my nurse now and so, alas all too soon, Dear Reader, must the time come for us to part. Toilsome was our journeying together, even as our going hence; but it is done. To me you were a beloved shade, the disembodied spirit of a friend. To you I was but a Warning Voice. Yet was our relation a kind of sacred one; doubt not that! Farewell!

Excellent Remedies for Various Ailments

To Cure the Toothache

1. A cat's skin is a good remedy for toothache. You should keep a dried cat's skin and hold it to your cheek when your tooth aches.

2. Carry in your pocket the two jaw-bones of a haddock; for ever since the miracle of the loaves and fishes these bones are an infallible remedy against toothache, and the older they are the better, as nearer the time of the miracle.

3. Put your finger on the fifth nail from the handle of the church door and say the creed three times.

Avoiding Bites and Stings

The addition of a little oil of eucalyptus or oil of bergamot to the morning bath will help in no small way to ward off the attentions of insects which annoy human beings. It is also a good plan to rub into the skin a little oil of lavender, or oil of pennyroyal, or oil of cloves.

When cycling, an excellent method of keeping away the gnats is to wash the hands and face in vinegar and water.

Two Cures for Baldness

1. Let calcine a raven. His ashes boil in sheep's suet. Rub to the head and it cures.

2. With mice fill an earthen pipkin. Stop the mouth with a lump of clay and bury beside a fire, but so as the fire's too great heat reach it not. So it be left for a year and at a year's end take out whatsoever may be found therein. But it is urgent that he that lift it have a glove upon his hand lest at his fingers' ends the hair come sprouting out.

Arsenic Cures

Arsenic has long been reputed one of the most violent poisons hitherto known, yet there is good reason to believe it bids fair to hold a place among the best and most valuable medicines.

The arsenic solution I have administered to adults—from ten drops twice a day to more than double that number thrice a day—have cured agues both by the extreme and all the intermediate doses. Large doses, however, three times a day, are found to be most efficacious.

Accordingly, I have drawn up the following table.

A Table of the Doses of Arsenic Solution

	Age	*Drops*
From	2 to 4 to take from	2 or 3 to 5
From	5 to 7	5–7
	8 to 12	7–10
	13 to 18	10–12
	18 & upwards	12

To be taken three times a day at six o'clock, two o'clock and ten o'clock.

To Stop Bleeding

1. For staunching blood: Take a fine full-grown toad; kill him, then take three bricks and keep in a very hot oven until they are red hot.

Take one out and place the toad upon it; when the brick is cold remove the toad; then take the other bricks and place the toad on them successively until he be reduced to powder.

Then take the toad-ashes and sew them up carefully in a silk bag one and a half inch square. When one is bleeding place this bag on the heart of the sufferer, and it will instantly stay the bleeding of the nose or any wound.

2. For stopping haemorrhage: As spitting of blood, bleeding from the nose, bleeding from a wound, etc., the following charm must be solemnly repeated once, twice, or oftener, according to the urgency of the case, by some old man or woman accounted more sagacious than their neighbours. It must not be repeated out loud, nor in the presence of any one but the patient:

> Three virgins came over Jordan's land
> Each with a bloody knife in her hand
> Stem, blood, stem—Letherly stand
> Bloody nose (or mouth) in God's name mend.

3. For spitting of blood: Take the dung of mice, beat it to a powder, put as much as will lie upon a sixpence in a quarter pint of juice of plantane, and sweeten with a little sugar. Give it in a morning, fasting, and at night going to bed. Continue this for some time and it will complete the cure.

4. To staunch bleeding: Cut an ash of one, two, or three years' growth, at the very hour and minute of the sun's entering into Taurus: a chip of this applied will stop bleeding.

When King James II was at Salisbury, his nose bled near two days, and after many essays in vain, was stopped by this sympathetic ash, which Mr William Nash, a surgeon in Salisbury, applied.

5. If a spider be put in a linen cloth a little bruised and holden to the nose that bleeds (but touch not the nose therewith, but smell to the same) by and by the blood will stay, and the nose will leave bleeding.

This is very true for the venomous spider is such an enemy to man's blood, that the blood draws back, and shuns the spider presently. A marvellous thing.

A Word about Gout

If it be any satisfaction to men in misery to be accounted amongst the number of those who are men of sense, all people who are afflicted with the *gout* may claim that privilege: for, for my own part, I never yet met with one *blockhead* or *fool* that was ever troubled with it.

The *blood*'s abounding with too great a quantity of *alkalious particles* is the general cause of this distemper, in order to which there are several other things which concur: As,

First: Too moist a state of air, which hinders free transpiration.

Secondly: The use of many sorts of meat, and too great ingurgitation thereof.

Thirdly: The often use of strong wines. Therefore it is well said,

> *He that in health would long remain,*
> *From drinking healths he must refrain.*

Fourthly: The immoderate use of venereal exercises, for that it spendeth the spirits and decayeth natural heat. Everybody experienceth that by a few venereal embraces his spirits become more languid, and his body more weakened, than by the loss of a large quantity of blood. It has been observed that few or none are ever troubled with the gout before marriage, or the use of venery.

Fifthly: Overmuch sleep, especially in the afternoon, and that immediately after dinner.

Sixthly: Overmuch watching and fasting and study and sorrow and care and much labour, because they spend the body.

Seventhly: Overmuch rest and ease.

Eighthly: Sudden rest and exposing the body to the air in cold or moist seasons after any violent exercise.

Ninthly: The total leaving off of any accustomed exercise.

Tenthly: From the keeping of the feet either too hot or too cold.

Eleventhly: From the stopping of any usual evacuation, as the monthly courses in women and a flux of the haemorrhoids in men, by means of which obstruction the excrementious matter wanting its usual vent is transmitted to some other part of the body.

The Medicinal Qualities of Tobacco

As a medicine tobacco is exhibited in various forms.

1. In substance. When chewed it causes an increased flow of saliva and sometimes relieves the toothache.

2. In infusion of water or wine it proves powerfully diuretic. An infusion is not more than 30 grams in 12 ounces of boiling water, and is often given in obstinate constipation and incarcerated hernia.

3. In the form of smoke it is injected into the anus by means of a bellows of a peculiar construction. By acting as a stimulus to the rectum, it sometimes succeeds in reviving the vital powers in some kinds of asphyxia, and in evacuating the intestines in cases of obstinate constipation.

A Universal Remedy

A universal cure for any native poison can be prepared from the wing-bone of a goose, the horn of the wild goat, the spine of the sea porcupine, and various yet unidentified jungle roots and barks. These are to be rubbed down in hot water and carefully strained before administration.

In the case of snake bite this sovereign remedy is to be applied first to the top of the head and then to the wound before it is swallowed by the patient. A powerful charm must be said at the same time.

The Wonders of the Air-Bath

To promote the due discharge of perspiratory matter—much of which, in old people and in disease, is azotic or putrescent—the air-bath should be used.

The best time for the air-bath, or naked exposure of the body, is on a sunny and dry day, when the barometer descends because of the increased weight of air. The greater the weight of dry air upon the body, the more braced and vigorous we will be; but when the air is charged with vapour and moist the body becomes languid, relaxed and feeble, then an exposure to the air-bath is by no means advisable.

In the open and clean air of the morning, great is the perspiration from the skin and lungs, especially if quickened by walking, running, riding or garden or field work; but if outdoor exercise cannot be had, labour within doors by swinging leads, one in each hand, by pulling dumb-bells or riding on a chamber-horse.

Secondly: Skip so as that the feet just clear the ground, throwing out the arms and instantly bringing them back. This exercise may be used either with or without a skipping cord.

Thirdly: Curtsey quickly and often, bending the knees to the ground, at the same time raising and sinking the arms.

Fourthly: While standing, bend the knees in and out alternately, but curtsey not: this motion greatly strengthens the ankles.

A Painless Method for Curing Piles

During an inflammatory attack of piles it is prudent as well as often necessary to observe the recumbent position until tenderness and inflammation subside, and strict attention during that time should be paid to diet. No liquid aliment other than barley water, toast and water, jelly and water, or weak tea with a little milk in it, may be drunk. Animal food should be sparingly partaken of, and consist of a small portion of boiled chicken or mutton or sole, with vegetables, and a light milk pudding; toast or bread and butter for tea and breakfast, and a supper of beef-tea and bread.

Patients should observe rigorously to avoid taking any of the following articles of diet, namely: fat, skin, bacon, pork, ham, pork sausages, rich cakes, greasy gravies, rich soups, entreés, pastry, much butter; also beer, spirits, sherry, port, champagne, and all effervescing drinks, but more especially beer and fat. Such aliments are literally poisonous and seriously increase the disease of piles.

Patients who give way to anger, fear or grief, seriously increase the complications of piles, and should, therefore, exercise a manly control over their passions if they are desirous of regaining health.

I am now desirous of bringing before the patient's notice the important and absolute necessity of using an electric magnetic battery of a continuous current, for a short time daily. The most useful and manageable of the kind to be recommended works with a crank or handle, which the patient attaches to the box containing the machinery. This handle the patient may turn himself, and regulate the strength of the current by the speed.

The size of the battery should be eight or nine inches in length. The method of using it is to place the right-hand insulator of the machine under the feet, in warm water; the left-hand insulator may be held with a dry piece of paper

round it, as a non-conductor, with a sponge inserted in the hollow, to prevent pricking sensations, and applied directly over the valve of the colon—the primary and absolute seat of the disease—for a quarter of an hour daily. Ten minutes should then be devoted to using the battery over the lower part of the abdomen, the sigmoid flexure of the colon, back and front of the liver, down the spine from the shoulders to the exterior of the anus.

A battery of the foregoing description is most simple and manageable, perfectly safe, agreeable to the senses, producing only a slight shaking motion. It may, in fact, be looked forward to with indifference if not pleasure.*

A Remedy for Melancholy

Melancholic patients should cultivate an entire change for the mind. Light amusements are most beneficial and much good has often been obtained by a good laugh at a farce, a thoroughly amusing book, a sea voyage, visits to the law courts, concerts, a hand at composition, church work and visiting, gardening, the care of pet animals—anything, in fact, to induce a disposition for a hobby of some kind; but, above all, an agreeable and sympathetic companion who will make it their study to talk with and amuse the patients, who, in general, have not strength of mind sufficient to overcome their despondency and depression.

No other diet can be better recommended than that stated for piles. The battery should be used daily over the liver, spine and lower part of the abdomen for twenty minutes. A mild anti-bilious pill may be taken every week for the first month,

---

* NOTE—Patients should not apply the current of the machine to other parts than those stated. The head, eyes, mouth, heart, upper part of spine, neck, lungs, pit of stomach, are all delicate and vital organs, and require special medical, not domestic treatment. Neither will such applications in any way effect the cure of piles.

but the chief cure lies in the application of the battery, combined with careful diet and diversion of the mind.

Cures for Whooping Cough

Some years ago it was found that the smell of gas-works is favourable for whooping cough, and children suffering from that troublesome complaint were taken to gas-works, which relieved them. Now the report comes from Illinois that they take children there who suffer from whooping cough down the shaft of the nearest coal mine and keep them there until cured.

The Proper Use of the Warm Bath

The proper time for the use of the Warm Bath is any time for an hour after breakfast till dinner; in those cases bathing may be continued for fifteen to twenty minutes, according to the feelings of the bather.

The sensation of the Warm Bath is exceedingly grateful to most persons, and the practice is universally safe; it may be employed at all seasons of the year and in all weathers, without danger or inconvenience.

Count Rumford has published an interesting essay on the subject of Warm Bathing, in which he observes that 'a person may gain fresh health, activity and spirits by bathing every day at two o'clock in the afternoon, at the temperature of 96 or 97 degrees Fahrenheit, and remaining in the Bath half an hour'. He continued the plan for thirty-five days and derived from it permanent advantage.

How to Cure a Madman

Hold him under water until he is almost drowned, then put him to bed in a dark room and his diet only milk pottage, half water.

The Alcoholic Cured

The tincture of capsicum in ten-drop doses is the best remedy to counteract that craving for alcohol which is the curse of all inebriates, preventing their return to rational conduct. This remedy has been tested by other physicians and they report very favourably in regard of it. They give several instances of men of various ages who, half muddled, hung around low drinking saloons or at home, when the liquor was shut up, would pick the lock, or when money was taken from them would tipple on credit whenever they had a chance.

The best way to administer this remedy is to commence with five drops in a little syrup of orange peel before meals, increasing the dose of capsicum tincture to twelve drops. In one month most of them became quite other men, changing from half idiots to men who attended to their business and took an interest in all that was going on in the world, which they before, being confirmed drunkards, did not.

A Remedy for Sleeplessness

To produce sleep:

First, to eat raw onions;

or

Second, because in a sleepless person the blood is in the brain and not in the stomach, to call the blood down by eating a few hard-boiled eggs, followed by a glass of rum or milk,

and you will fall asleep.

The Importance of Fresh Air

In recent years a great change has come over the opinion of educated people as to the necessity of a plentiful supply of fresh air and of the provision of really adequate ventilation of our rooms if we are to keep in health, but still nine people out of ten are as afraid as ever of fresh air, and especially of what they call 'night' air. The early morning atmosphere of the rooms in which many people sleep is foul beyond description.

Sewage flowing into pure water pollutes it. So the air we exhale from our lungs pollutes the air in the room. The impure air from the lungs of any number of people in a room mixes with the pure air, and makes it dangerous and unfit for breathing. All the air in a room, ten feet long, ten feet wide, and ten feet high, is sufficient only for one person for twenty minutes; and, if no fresh air is admitted, the person occupying such a room must breathe his own breath over and over again until its degree of pollution amounts to the poisonous.

It is impossible to estimate the amount of misery and suffering caused by impure air. There is no doubt that much of what is called morning laziness—that is to say, waking up tired—is due solely to the fact that the previous eight hours or so have been spent in an atmosphere almost poisonous, for air that has already been breathed is not only harmful by reason of the abstraction of oxygen from it, and the addition to it of carbonic acid gas, but also from the decomposing organic matter which is continually being given off by the skin and lungs. Foul air is undoubtedly the commonest pre-disposing cause of influenza, pneumonia and consumption.

→ Essential Etiquette ←

The Market Value of Good Manners

I want you to think of this world as a very large market, in which each of us has his particular form of merchandise to dispose of. It may be goods such as coal and cotton, or brains, or physical strength, or manual skill. Whatever it be, it is for sale, and its market value goes up when the supply is less than the demand, and down when the reverse is the case.

And yet, however clever you may be, however skilful your hand, whatever the quality of your goods, success or failure depends to a great extent upon other qualities.

Let us consider the cases of A, B, C and D.

Each takes a shop in the same street, sells the same goods and the same quality of goods.

A has bad health, and cannot attend regularly to his business; B regards work as something to be avoided whenever possible, and takes a good many holidays when he ought to be in his shop; C works hard enough and has capital health, but he is a surly fellow and never puts himself out on anybody's account; D works hard and has very good health, and is pleasant and obliging to everybody.

In a few months A and B find they have to shut up their shops, because the others have qualities in which they are lacking; later on, C thinks he would do better in another street, as D is taking away many of his customers.

Why? Because he has a most important quality which C has not.

Hence, whatever merchandise we have to put on the world's market, we must, if we wish to succeed, have health to enable us to do our work, energy and perseverance to enable us to fight our way, and good manners to show our goods to the best advantage.

The market value of good manners cannot be quoted like that of coal, eggs or fruit. The reason is, that good manners are not so much a form of merchandise as an essential quality in the merchant.

Bad manners will hinder your success in life, just as a badly arranged and dirty shop-window hinders a business, by sending customers to other shops which are cleaner and neater, and which consequently make them much more pleasant to deal with.

The Importance of Conformity

You must conform, to such an extent as not to annoy and give offence to the customs, whether in dress or other matter, of

the circle in which you move. This conformity is an implied condition in the social compact. It is a practical recognition of the rights of others and shows merely a proper regard for their opinions and feelings.

If you cannot adapt your dress and manners to the company in which you find yourself, the sooner you take your leave the better.

How to Converse in Society

The use of slang phrases or crack words should be carefully avoided. Nothing can be more detrimental to the advancement of those who desire to acquire colloquial polish than the habit of using inelegant language. Good, pure English must commend itself to all but the vulgar and the pedantic.

The advantage of habitual practice cannot be too highly recommended to those who would acquire colloquial skill. But while fluency and ease are the results of practice, the embellishments of conversation require careful culture. Humour and repartee, though to some extent natural gifts, may undoubtedly be improved, if not attained, by artificial training.

Sheridan prepared himself for convivial occasions like an intellectual gladiator, ready to enter the lists in a valiant struggle for supremacy. He made brief notes before going into society of appropriate topics and witticisms for each occasion, upon which he relied for sustaining his reputation as an accomplished talker.

But if one would not desire preparation as elaborately artificial as that ascribed to this spoiled fondling of the aristocracy, there seems to be a propriety in making some mental as well as external arrangements before entering society.

Thus, to reflect upon the general character of the company one is to meet and upon the subjects most appropriate for conversation with those with whom one will probably be individually associated, may not be amiss.

Happily, however, for those who distrust their power to surprise by erudition or delight by wit, good sense, accompanied by good humour and courtesy, render their possessors the most enduringly agreeable of social and domestic companions.

Onions, etc.

All food or drinks which taint the breath or cause disagreeable eructations should be avoided by persons going into company. Onions emit so disagreeable an odour that no truly polite person will eat them when liable to inflict their fumes upon others.

When to Make an Introduction

It is neither necessary nor desirable to introduce everybody to everybody, and the promiscuous presentations sometimes inflicted upon us are anything but agreeable.

You also put yourself in an unpleasant position, for 'an introduction is a social endorsement' and you have become, to a certain extent, responsible for the person you introduce. If he disgraces himself in any way, you share in his disgrace.

As a general rule, no gentleman should be presented to a lady without her permission being previously obtained. Between gentlemen this formality is not always necessary, but you should have good reason to believe that the acquaintance will be agreeable to both, before introducing any persons to each other.

If you are walking with a friend and are met or joined by another, it is not necessary to introduce them to each other; but you may do so if you think they would be glad to become acquainted.

The inferior should be introduced to the superior—the gentleman to the lady, as, 'Miss Brown, permit me to introduce Mr Smith.'

However, if you are a gentleman, do not, we beg you, permit the lack of an introduction to prevent you from promptly offering your services to any unattended lady who may need them. Take off your hat and politely beg the honour of protecting, escorting or assisting her and when the service has been accomplished, bow and retire.

How to Converse with Ladies

Respecting conversations with ladies, though all mere silliness and twaddle should be regarded as equally unworthy of them and yourselves, yet, in their society, agreeability rather than profundity should be your aim in the choice of topics. Playfulness, cheerfulness, versatility and courtesy should characterise colloquial intercourse with ladies; but the deference due to them should never degenerate into mere servile acquiescence or mawkish sentimentality.

The utmost refinement of language and of matter should always be regarded as essential, under such circumstances, to the discourse of a well-bred man, and should, of course, distinguish his manner as well. Thus, all slang phrases, everything approaching *double entendre*, all familiarity of address unsanctioned by relationship or acknowledged intimacy, all mistimed or unsanctioned use of nicknames and Christian names, are as inadmissible in good society as are personal familiarities—nudging, winking, whispering, etc.

The discourtesy sometimes exhibited by young men towards ladies and clergymen, in the use of equivocal language and the introduction of exceptionable subjects in their hearing, cannot be too highly condemned.

Anything that will crimson the cheek of true womanhood, or invade the unconsciousness of innocence, is unworthy and unmanly to a degree of which it is not easy to find language to express sufficient abhorrence. The defencelessness of the dependent sex in this, as in other respects, is their best protection, in the eyes of a manly character.

Pulling out One's Watch

Pulling out your watch in company, unasked, either at home or abroad, is a mark of ill-breeding. If at home, it appears as if you were tired of your company and wished them to be gone; if abroad, as if the hours dragged heavily and you wished to be gone yourself.

If you want to know the time, withdraw.

A Word on Posture and Bearing

Crossing the legs, elevating the feet, lounging on one side, looking back, etc. though quite excusable in the abandon of bachelor seclusion, should never be indulged in where ceremony is properly required.

Early acquire the habit of standing and walking with your chest thrown out, your head erect, your abdomen receding, rather than protruding, a self-poised and firm but elastic tread and altogether a compact, manly homogeneous sort of bearing and movement.

In the company of ladies, particularly, too much care cannot be exhibited in one's attitudes. It is then proper to sit upright with the feet on the floor and the hands quietly readjusted before one, either holding the hat or stick (as when paying a morning visit) or the dress-hat carried in the evening; or, to give ease, on occasion, a book, roll of paper or the like. Habits of refinement once established, a man feels at ease; he can trust himself, without watching, to be natural; and nothing conduces more to grace and elegance than this quiet consciousness.

The Correct Arrangement of the Male Organs

Carry your sexual organs towards the left thigh, where Nature makes the largest place for them.

Gloves

In shaking hands it is more respectful to offer an ungloved hand; but if two gentlemen are both gloved, it is very foolish to keep each other waiting to take them off.

You should not, however, offer a gloved hand to a lady or a superior who is ungloved. If your glove be dark-coloured or your hand ungloved, do not offer to shake hands with a lady in full dress.

Stairs

In ascending or descending stairs with a lady, it is proper to offer your arm, provided the stair-case is sufficiently wide to permit two to go up or down abreast.

But if it is not, which should go first?

It is a general rule of etiquette to give ladies the precedence everywhere, but if you follow a lady in going upstairs, she might display a large foot or a thick ankle which were better concealed.

Let the ladies decide.

On the Street

Except in a case of necessity, you should not stop a business man on the street during business hours. He may have appointments, and, in any event, his time is precious. If you must speak with him, walk on in his direction; or if you detain him, state your errand briefly and politely apologise for the detention.

When you meet a lady with whom you are acquainted, you should lift your hat as you bow to her; but it is the lady's duty to give some sign of recognition first, as she might *possibly* choose to 'cut' you, and thus place you in a very awkward position; but unless you have forfeited all claims to respect, she certainly should do no such a thing.

If you wish to speak with a lady whom you meet on the street, turn and walk with her, but you should not accompany her far, except at her request, and should always lift your hat and bow upon withdrawing.

How to Host a Dinner Party

Three things are required to give an enjoyable dinner party: good taste, good judgement and an intuitive sense of harmony. Nervousness, annoyance, anxiety on the part of the host or hostess during the serving of the dinner, are the deadly foes of enjoyment. The chief charm of a dinner party lies in ease of manner on the part of the host and hostess, and when the first guest is announced they should cast aside all responsibility, and act as if it were indeed a festive occasion. There is nothing so conducive to indigestion as a face of woe and anxiety at the head or foot of the table. If anything goes wrong, do not notice it, unless it is shockingly glaring; in this case, if possible, pass it off with a jest.

To ensure the success of a dinner party the company must be carefully selected. As far as practicable the guests should be acquainted with each other, and likely to harmonise in general conversation. Nothing is more trying than to have to sit through a dinner next to a person whose company is neither congenial nor entertaining, and who is possibly either crotchety or egotistical. An equal number of ladies and gentlemen should be invited, but not more than the table will accommodate with comfort, allowing at least sixteen inches of room to each person. The flowers should be quite fresh and tastefully arranged. The room should be well lighted and everything appear as bright and cheerful as possible. The napery should be snow-white, and the table appointments generally as attractive as means will permit without being ostentatious.

Invitations to a dinner party should be issued in the names of both host and hostess about three weeks before the actual date, and etiquette involves the necessity of a prompt reply.

How to Eat

Among minor characteristics, few are so indicative of genuine good breeding as a man's mode of eating.

It is of importance to learn to sit uprightly at table, to keep one's individual 'aids and appliances' compactly arranged; to avoid all noise and hurry in the use of these conveniences; neither to mince nor fuss with one's food.

Eating with a knife or with the fingers; soiling the lips; using the fork or the fingers as a tooth-pick; making audible the process of mastication or of drinking; taking soup from the point of a spoon; lolling forward upon the table or with the elbows upon the table; soiling the cloth with what should be kept on the plate; in short, everything that is odd or coarse should nowhere be indulged in.

Should you have occasion for a tooth-pick, hold your napkin or your hand before your mouth while applying it: and on no account resort to the perceptible assistance of the tongue in freeing the mouth or teeth from food.

Have sufficient self-control when so unfortunate as to be disgusted with anything in your food to refrain from any outward manifestation of annoyance, and, if possible, to conceal from others all participation in your discovery.

DELICIOUS RECIPES FOR DISCERNING CHEFS

Sugar Mice

Begin by skinning the mouse, which should be caught in an ordinary mousetrap; empty them and tie them by the tail to a wooden spoon. Then drop them into a strong sugar syrup in a cast iron saucepan over a slow heat. After some hours (or days) the mice become crystallised and, when they are cold, they are ready to eat.

They are *delicious* and even the bones are crisp and edible (not unlike the bones in a mature tin of sardines). You will never have chest trouble if you eat such sweetmeats.

A Hunter's Breakfast

When the larger animals of the wilderness fall before the hunter's rifle the resources of the African *chef de cuisine* are really called into requisition. Suppose an elephant has been laid low, and, after an extemporised supper of steaks, or 'carbonatjies', the party determine to have a foot for breakfast, the fire, which has already partially dried the ground is swept away, or perhaps a new spot is chosen, and a hole thirty inches in width and depth is made, a fire is lighted in this, and a quantity of dry wood thrown on and allowed to burn until the sides of the hole and the earth immediately surrounding it are thoroughly heated; the fire is then raked out, the foot, generally a fore one, which has been amputated at what may be called the wrist-joint, and answering to the knee of the horse, is placed in its natural position in it, the ashes are shovelled in, the hot embers above them, the hot earth over all, and a roaring fire is lighted on the top and left to burn all night.

In the morning this is cleared off, the foot is dug out, the upper parts soiled by the contact of the ashes are cut away, and the rich gelatine and other morsels are left to be dug out by the stout keen pointed knives of the expectant hunters, the tough skin serving all the purposes of a dish. Very frequently a piece of the trunk is put in at the same time, and this is generally left as a stand-by, to be eaten cold, when it looks and tastes almost like coarse tongue; the foot, on the contrary, being best while still warm.

Turtle Soup

Take the turtle from the water the evening before it is wanted, lay it on its back in the morning, tie its feet, cut off the head, and hang it up to bleed. Remove the scales and cut it open, take out all the meat, soak the white meat by itself in salt and water, cut off the fins, keep them separate, keep the *inside* or gut separate also, put all the refuse meat into a soup pot, with sufficient water, a turnip, carrot, celery, parsley, a few onions and a bunch of sweet herbs, including a predominance of basil, a seasoning of mace, nutmeg, cloves, salt and white pepper; boil them gently for three hours.

The gut having been cut up and well washed is simmered until quite tender, and cut into narrow strips; the white meat is stewed with the lungs and heart, cut into small square pieces, reserving a portion for cutlets. Add these to the strained soup, and also a portion of the green fat of the turtle, and thicken with arrowroot; add half a pint of wine, a dozen forcemeat balls, also a dozen egg balls. Turtle fins make a nice corner dish.

Raw Meat Juice

Raw meat juice is best made from rump steak. The meat should be very finely minced, and put into a jar with a little salt and just enough cold water to cover it completely, and should be left thus to stand for an hour.

The meat should then be strained off in a piece of clean, fine muslin, and pounded with a pestle and mortar until everything possible is expressed from the meat fibre into the water. The juice can, of course, be made stronger or weaker according to the amount of water added.

This meat juice requires to be prepared freshly every time it is used, as it does not keep well; and in the case of a fastidious invalid it is best given in a covered feeding-cup.

Brain Fritters

Soak the brain in salt water to remove the blood. Skin. Place in cold salted water, bring to the boil and simmer for ten minutes or until cooked. Allow to cool and cut into fairly thick slices. Dip in fritter batter and fry in deep fat.

Roast Tongue and Udder

The udder eats well boiled with the tongue. Let the tongue be well cleaned and salted, after which it must lie three days; then boil it with a fine young udder that has some fat adhering thereto. When tolerably tender, roast the whole together, baste them with red wine, and froth them nicely with a bit of butter. Serve up to table with gravy and good currant jelly sauce, first sticking into the udder ten or twelve cloves.

Bear Rump Roast

Use about an eight pound roast off the rump of a young bear. Cover with cold water, add three or four medium-sized onions (sliced), and let soak about four hours (cubs will need about two and a half hours cooking). Remove from water and wipe dry. Cut one small clove garlic into small pieces and, using a sharp knife to make holes, force garlic deep into meat. Get

garlic as near bones as possible. Season with salt and pepper. Brown in hot bacon drippings. Bake in open pan for three hours at 350 degrees Fahrenheit, turning the meat several times while cooking.

How to Cook a Hippopotamus

Where hippopotami have never been fired at they are very tame and even inquisitive. I remember finding a herd in a small rock-pool on the Lower Umfuli, which, probably, had never seen a man with any kind of clothes on before, as they showed no fear whatever, but all came up within a few yards of me and remained with their heads in full view for a long time, staring stolidly at the unwonted sight and continually twitching their little ears.

Towards the end of the rainy season, about March or April in South Africa, hippopotami become excessively fat and the meat of a young cow in good condition is exceedingly good; in my opinion better than that of any antelope. An old bull is, of course, always very tough and usually very lean. Hippo meat is dark red in colour and in flavour more resembles beef than pork.

Hippopotami are usually killed by a shot in the brain as they raise their heads above the surface of the water to breathe. It is as well to take time and try and make sure of the first shot. When killed by a shot in the brain, a hippopotamus at once sinks to the bottom and if the water is cold and deep the carcase will not rise to the surface for six hours or sometimes longer. When the water is warm the carcase will rise in about three hours.

A mode of cooking a dish of hippopotamus, discovered by Sir Samuel Baker, is well worth bearing in mind. Speaking of it, he says: 'I tried boiling the fat flesh and skin together, the result being that the skin assumed the appearance of the green fat of the turtle, but is far superior. A piece of the head thus boiled and then soused in vinegar, with chopped onions and cayenne pepper and salt, throws brawn completely in the shade.'

Seventeen Squirrels in a Pot

Take seventeen squirrels, three cans tomato sauce, two pounds onions, chopped, two heads garlic, four stalks chopped celery, two bell peppers, chopped, cooking oil, four tablespoons flour, salt and pepper to taste. Cut up meat. Salt and pepper. Brown meat in pot with one-eighth-inch cooking oil. Add small amounts of water from time to time to prevent sticking.

Remove meat when tender. Make small roux in large pot with oil and flour (four tbsps). Add onions and small amount of water if they stick, cook until tender. Add bell peppers, garlic and celery. Add tomato sauce and extra water if it becomes too thick. Simmer until vegetables are tender. Add squirrels and simmer until oil comes to top. Salt and pepper to taste. Serve over rice.

Crunchy Frogs

The only legitimate way to cook a frog is to fry him brown in sweet table butter. As a preliminary he must be dipped in a batter of cracker dust, which should adhere closely when cooked forming a dainty cracknel of a golden brown colour,

with a crisp tang to it when submitted to the teeth. The tender juices thus retained lose none of their delicate flavour.

Next to the pleasure of sitting on the borders of a frog-pond at eventide and listening to their sweet, melancholy *ch-r-r-rk* is that of reviewing a plate heaped high with the mementoes of a finished feast—the bones of the 'Frog that would a-wooing go' and a goodly portion of his kindred.

How to Cook and Eat a Live Goose

Take a goose or a duck, or some such 'lively creature' (but a goose is the best of all for this purpose), pull off all her feathers, only the head and the neck must be spared; then make a fire round about her, not too close to her, that the smoke do not choke her, and that the fire may not burn her too soon: nor too far off, that she may not escape free; within the circle of the fire let there be set small cups and pots full of water, wherein salt and honey are mingled; and let there be set also chargers full of sodden-apples, cut into small pieces in the dish.

The goose must be all larded, and basted over with butter, to make her the more fit to be eaten, and may roast the better:

put then fire about her, but do not make too much haste, when as you see her begin to roast; for by walking about, and flying here and there, being cooped in by the fire that stops her way out, the unwearied goose is kept in; she will fall to drink the water to quench her thirst and cool her heart, and all her body, and the apple sauce will make her dung, and cleanse and empty her. And when she roasteth, and consumes inwardly, always wet her head and heart with a wet sponge; and when you see her giddy with running, and begin to stumble, her heart wants moisture, and she is roasted enough. Take her up, set her before your guests, and she will cry as you cut off any part from her, and will be almost eaten up before she be dead; it is mighty pleasant to behold.

❧ FLAWLESS BEAUTY TIPS ❧
FOR PLAIN PEOPLE

How to Stay Young

Past grief, old angers, revenges, even past pleasures, constantly dwelt upon—all dead, decaying or decayed thought—make a sepulchre of the soul, a cemetery of the body and a weather-beaten monument of the face. This is age.

The women who never grow old are the student women—those who daily drink in new chyle* through memorising, thoroughly analysing and perfectly assimilating subjects apart from themselves. Study is development—is eternal youth. The student woman who makes wise use of her acquisitions has no time to corrugate her brow with dread thought of the beauty-destroyer leaping fast behind her.

Neither considered nor invited, old age keeps his distance. Brain culture, based on noble motive, means sympathy, heart gentleness, charity, graciousness, enlargement of sense, feeling, power. Such a being cannot become a fossil.

* Juice. Late Latin *chylus* from the Greek *khulos* ('juice') [Ed.].

Bathing Beauties

No woman can be beautiful who does not take her bath regularly. Poisons are retained in the body, the skin is never smooth nor healthy and the complexion never clear. A woman who powders, paints and enamels her face will eventually spoil her natural complexion completely; but by frequent bathing she will improve and preserve her good looks. Use pure white Castile soap and a flesh brush, softening the water, if hard, with a tablespoonful of borax for each gallon.

Baths in which milk, bran or starch has been placed are found to refine or whiten the coarsest, reddest skin if persistently used. Softness and firmness of skin may be obtained by the use of a simple unguent made famous by the Greek and Roman women, who centuries ago set us the example of perfect personal cleanliness as the road to beauty. The following can be made with very little trouble and it is delightfully exhilarating after the bath. Best white vinegar one pint, rosemary, rue, camphor and lavender (of each) two drachms. Let the herbs soak in the vinegar for several hours, then strain. Rub thoroughly all over the body and a deliciously comfortable feeling and a dainty perfume will remain with one all day long.

Washing the Hair

Don't wash the hair more than once a month. Do not use soap, but the yolk of a new-laid egg in rain or river water.

To Remove Freckles

To remove freckles use the following:

One ounce lemon juice
Quarter drachm powdered borax
Half drachm pulverised sugar.

Mix all, let it stand in a glass for a few days, then apply it and let it dry on the skin.

Or: Apply with a linen cloth two tablespoonfuls of grated horseradish mixed with a teacupful of sour milk.

The nose is very apt to freckle, but these little brown spots can be removed by putting on the nose a little of this lotion:

Lemon juice, three ounces
Vinegar, one ounce
Rose-water, one ounce
Jamaica rum, one ounce.

Apply this with a sponge several times a day.

When the face is washed care must be taken to dry the nose downward, not upward, and whenever the nose is touched with the hand or handkerchief, the same advice must be borne in mind or very ugly results will follow.

Banishing Black Spots

For banishing black spots, an excellent ointment is made of

Flowers of sulphur, one teaspoonful
Rose-water, one pint
Glycerine, one teaspoonful.

If the specks are very obstinate and hard to remove this preparation should be used:

Liquid ammonia, twenty drops
Ether, one drachm
Soft soap, one ounce.

Bathe the place affected with hot water and then rub in a little of this mixture with the ball of the thumb. Then wash it off with hot water.

Here is another remedy for black spots:

Dilute a tablespoonful of gin with two tablespoonfuls of cold water. Wash the face regularly with this night and morning, mixing it fresh each time.

A Word of Advice Regarding Corsets

Well-made, properly fitting, skilfully-cut corsets are indispensable to a woman who wishes to be well dressed and preserve a good figure. No dress will look well over a badly-cut, ill-fitting pair of corsets, and the effect of the most beautiful and expensive gown may be utterly spoilt by inattention to this important detail of feminine attire. If a good make is selected there should be no difficulty in obtaining a perfect fit for almost any figure, and no discomfort or ill-effects need be feared from wearing corsets of this kind.

When one recalls the injurious effects which have undoubtedly resulted from the wearing of tight corsets, it seems a little surprising to find one of our leading medical journals going out of its way to defend this garment. But there are corsets and corsets, and though, as the *British Medical Journal* pointed out some time ago, there are a certain number of foolish women, young and old, who still make themselves miserable by wearing their things too tight, the average woman, at any rate of the well-to-do classes, is sensible on the subject.

It may be doubted whether those who argue that all clothes should be suspended from the shoulders really have science on their side. All shoulder dress-hanging arrangements pull as much forward as backward, and thus tend, unless the back muscles are kept constantly in action, to throw the pectoral muscles out of gear, and to contract the chest, by rendering full inspirations impossible. The heaviest part of a woman's dress is her skirt, and when hung from her hips and sacrum, its weight is transmitted straight through the hip-joints, knees and ankles to the ground, instead of through those same joints plus some sixteen others. It is true that men usually suspend their nether garments from their shoulders; but the first thing a man naturally does when about to take active exercise is to take off his braces and replace them by a real or improvised belt.

A further disadvantage which would attend the adoption by women of a form of dress which depended entirely upon shoulder suspension would be that it would almost certainly put an end to the popularity of the blouse. This would be a pity, for the blouse is, from the hygienic point of view, a particularly desirable form of garment. Even persons who are not well off can supply themselves with several, and change them as often as soiled. Still, this is very different from allowing that tight stays do anything but harm to both health and beauty.

But whilst the wearing of corsets is necessary in order to preserve a graceful figure, care should be taken that a sensible shape is selected. It is not every woman who can afford to have her corsets specially made by a Corsetiere, and for those who cannot, the best and most hygienic ready-made corset on the market is the 'J. B. Side-spring'. This is a corset built on scientific lines, and, by reason of the side-spring, will respond to every movement of the body. We would recommend every woman who cannot have her corsets specially made to wear 'J. B.' The prices are reasonable, from 3s. 11d. to 10s. 6d., and the corsets will be found to be much superior to others at much higher prices.

Removing Tartar

There is often a formation of tartar upon the teeth. For removing this incrustation Dr Scoffern recommends hydrochloric acid, strong, as obtained from the druggist. He says:

'The name of the liquid will sound frightful enough to a timid girl, but if employed in the way to be described no ill-effects will follow.

'The method of using is this: Procure a clean skewer—one of those used by butchers—hammer or batter out the sharp point of it into a very small brush, not larger than one of the small sable brushes used in miniature painting. Dip this into hydrochloric acid, allowing all superfluous acid to drain off, and rub the part of the tooth to be purified. There are very few incrustations which will resist this treatment.

'Care should be taken that, so soon as the operation is finished, all lingering traces of the acid be well removed from the mouth with chalk and water.'

For some time after the operation just described has been performed the teeth will feel rough, will 'be set on edge', to use a common expression, a sufficient indication of the destruction which must result from habitual recourse to the process.

How to Stop Blushing

Blushing will cure itself, if the young man or shy, modest maiden will only give up thinking about it. They should mix freely in the society of their friends of both sexes and by experience gain confidence. By putting themselves in the way of meeting the emotion which distresses and embarrasses them, and by a determination to overcome their nervousness, they will generally succeed.

The effort to regain composure and indifference to what onlookers think is more successful if certain rules be observed. A quick cold or coolish bath on rising, followed by a brisk towelling; the substitution of cocoa or milk for tea and coffee; daily indulgence in moderate outdoor exercise; regular hours for meals and sleep; and plain food, thoroughly chewed—all help. The bowels must act once a day. And if further assistance be required, a good nerve tonic may be taken.

For Tired Eyes

If the eyes are tired and burn, rest them and bathe them in the following simple yet excellent wash: To a quart of soft, boiled water add a tablespoonful of the best brandy and a teaspoonful of salt.

A Word about Chins

The chin should be round, white and well-modelled. Resolution and firmness are expressed by a well-formed chin, while weakness of disposition is shown in a retreating one. The author of a work on noses says that we may, in a very appreciable degree, form our own noses, and it is at least equally true that we can do much towards securing well-formed chins.

If circumstances favour the development of firmness in character, the chin improves steadily under those circumstances. If, on the contrary, weakness and irresolution and a tendency to be easily led by others become fixed in the nature and fostered by events, the chin retreats more and more in consonance with the deterioration of the will.

✦ Advice of a Delicate Nature ✦

Continence

Smoking and drinking are things that tempt some fellows and not others, but there is one temptation that is pretty sure to come to you at one time or another and I just want to warn you about it.

It is called in our schools 'beastliness', and that is about the best name for it.

Smoking and drinking and gambling are men's vices and therefore attract some boys, but this 'beastliness' is not a man's vice; men have nothing but contempt for a fellow who gives way to it.

Some boys, like those who start smoking, think it a very fine and manly thing to tell or listen to dirty stories, but it only shows them to be little fools.

Yet such talk and the reading of trashy books or looking at lewd pictures are very apt to lead a thoughtless boy into the temptations of self-abuse. This is a most dangerous thing for him, for, should it become a habit, it tends to destroy both health and spirits.

But if you have any manliness in you, you will throw off such temptation at once; you will stop looking at the books and listening to the stories and you will give yourself something else to think about.

Sometimes the desire is brought on by indigestion or from eating too rich food or from constipation. It can therefore be cured by correcting these and by bathing at once in cold water or by exercising the upper part of the body by arm exercises, boxing, etc.

If you still have trouble about it, do not make a secret of it, but go to your scoutmaster and talk it over with him, and all will come right.

Concerning 'Strange Women'

When a young fellow first comes to any of our large cities or towns he finds himself, so to speak, lost in the crowd, and feels free to do more or less as he likes. At home everybody knew him, and this very fact served as a restraint; but here no one does. And besides this he is now in lodgings, and has no friend's house where he can spend his evenings. He cannot afford to be going always to picture-palaces and places of amusement, so he strolls about the streets. He sees other young men and maidens meeting one another, and laughing and talking together, and longs for companionship and company.

Then too in the glare and glitter of the gaslight he sees girls of a certain class, walking alone, who smile and swish their skirts, and glance significantly at him over their shoulders as they pass in a way which sets his pulse beating. They are powdered and perfumed, decked out and dressed to allure and attract, and unless he is a youth of high moral principle and Christian character he is all too likely, sooner or later, to be led away of his own lust and enticed to follow some 'strange woman' to the house of ill-fame. But the house of the strange woman leads straight to death and hell.

You may see it all exemplified by the moth as it flutters round the light, and then, scorching its wings, falls with a dull thud upon the table; then recovering itself again, dashes blindly and madly once more into the flame; and then crawls into the dark and dies in agony in the dust.

Do I speak to one who has sometimes stood on the very verge of such a sin? If so, let him still tremble, and at the same time thank God he was prevented and preserved from it.

How to Choose a Wife

Advice to persons about to marry—'Don't!'
Punch (1845)

• *Do not think that the first female to whom you have the opportunity or the inclination of paying your addresses is the only one you can ever meet with that would make you a good wife.*

Some young men must make an offer to the first female that happens to take their fancy. 'Never have such a chance again', 'charming creature', 'the very one', 'Miss Right', and we know not what besides. Well they act accordingly, and what is the consequence? Why they sometimes find, when it is for ever too late, that if they had waited longer they might have done a great deal better.

• *Never marry whom you cannot love.*

Now and then young men are the victims of ardent but indiscreet attachment. When you are aware that your feelings are being excited and that love is waking, make haste to ask yourself some such questions as the following. Is she suitable?

Will it meet with the general sanction of true friends? Will it bear the test of public criticism? Is it a reasonable love or the excitement of a madcap? Can you always love her?

• *Correct domestic habits are essential.*

Nothing can redeem the want of good domestic qualities. With them you may be happy, without them you never can. Is the lady to whom you intend paying your addresses fond of house-keeping now? Is she domestic now? If she is not now, you have no reason to expect that she will be after your nuptials.

• *Seek a bride of good temper, amiable disposition, and modest bearing.*

An irritable, fretful, peevish, scolding dis-position is a misery to its possessor and it makes everybody miserable that it touches. There can be no peace where quarrelsome propensities are dominant. The house that echoes to these constant dissensions is more like a furious demo-cratic debating society than a happy home. Shakespeare speaks of Taming the Shrew, but the man that would attempt it, in a confirmed case, must have nerves of iron.

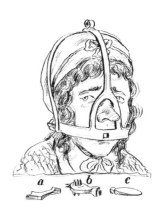

• *Marry your equal as nearly as you can.*

Wives whose positions in life were greatly inferior to those of their husbands are often meddlesome. On the other hand, to marry one far above you is quite as likely to cause you pain. Should she be opulent and you not rich, then, when the honey-moon is over, she may beg to remind you of her condescension in stooping to become your bride. A young man with any spirit in him would break stones on the road and earn his bread by the sweat of his brow rather than submit to such cruel and disgusting taunts.

• *Give a decided preference to polished manners and a cultivated mind.*

A young lady wilfully uneducated does not deserve a good husband, and it is not likely that she will get one. You may take it
for granted that she will not care much for the education of
her own offspring if she passed through an expensive process
of education without making any decided improvement. Polished manners are quite as requisite as mental acquirements.
In choosing a wife, seek for those good manners that proceed
from a good heart. Perpetual nausea and disgust will be your
doom if you marry a vulgar and uncultivated woman.

• *While we would not have you attach yourself to deformity, we
would caution you against marrying only for beauty.*

Do not be so silly as to marry a wife for the same reason that a
child buys a pretty doll, or an amateur purchases a fine painting or a splendid statue. You must seek sterling worth rather
than beauty. Beauty is a rare thing on earth, but beauty allied
to sterling worth is rarer still, and therefore you cannot all of
you have models of beauty for your wives. The majority of you
must either marry females of average appearance or remain
unmarried.

A Note about 'Popping' the Question

Girls say 'yes' to all questions 'popped' in a deep, rich, strong,
rumbling, powerful male voice, but they say 'no' to questions
popped in a weak, quackling, piping, thin, squeak-mouse,
gelding voice.

How to Spoil a Husband

A man's conduct, his morals, his general thrift are determined
by a variety of circumstances. But none among all the influences that act upon him is to be compared with the influence
of his wife.

A woman's influence is pervasive and continuous. Others have to gain access to him. She has a near place and the first chance always; the first in the morning and the last at night. She touches all the springs of life, through her children, through her domestic arrangements, through her personal attractions. She reaches his pride, his ambition, his temper, his love and his passions, as no other one may.

A wife can destroy her husband. She can soon dispel the marriage illusion that she was good, amiable and angelic. After a few days, let her manifest selfishness; study her own comfort and neglect his; meet his advances with rebuff; get him angry and torment him till he is furious; convince him that she cares for him only when she has some plan to carry. Let her see to it that the house is uncomfortable. Whenever any thing goes wrong, put the blame on him. Never give up on any question, watch his words and actions, and throw up to him every day, in the most provoking manner, his little mistakes. This will form a first-class receipt for ruining any common man. He will be sure to take his comfort somewhere away from home.

If his home is dreary, the drinking-shop is gay and genial. If his wife peppers him, all the more reason for spending as much time with jolly fellows who tell good stories, drink in good fellowship, and have a rousing good time generally! Then, the wife will have a good chance to excite sympathy in her behalf, as a poor neglected creature, and the husband will be duly regarded as a monster!

If a woman sets out, she can make home little better than a hell. But women do not need to pursue such a vulgar path to ruin. A wife may love her husband and her children and may perform her ordinary duties faithfully, and yet ruin her husband by her foolish ambition. She envies every one more prosperous than her husband is. She wishes a house a little beyond his means; she will have clothes not consistent with his income; she demands expensive pleasures which suck up his slender earnings; she brings him in debt, keeps him feverish with anxiety, and finally poisons his very honesty. Many a man breaks down in reputation and becomes a castaway under the stimulation of his wife's dishonest ambition. For, to live beyond one's means is dishonest.

Let a woman scatter faster than her husband can gather; let her secure the art of making home uncomfortable, and of tempting her husband to prefer any other place to it; let her use her husband as seamstresses do pin-cushions, to stick pins in; and, with ordinary luck, she will ruin any commonly clever fellow in a few years. Having driven him to a drunkard's grave, she can muffle her martyred heart under funeral-smelling crêpe and walk in comely black, until some new victim helps her put on again her wedding suit.

Building up Your Wife's Breasts

Have your wife's breasts declined since you courted and married her? It is because her womb has declined and nursing up her love will rebuild both her womb and breasts.

Come, court her up again as you used to before marriage and, besides reddening up her now pale cheeks, lightening her now lagging motion, you will redevelop her shrivelled breasts.

Stay home of nights from your club rooms, billiard saloons and lodges to read or talk to her or escort her to parties, lectures, concerts and you'll get well paid every time you see her bust.

⚔ Some Excellent Observations ⚔ on the Duties of Parenthood

Fitness for Parenthood

It is one of the cardinal principles of Eugenics that those with a bad family history should not become parents. Weak or abnormal mentality; chronic immorality or perverted moral sense; or diseased or abnormal physical conditions—these should always be regarded as bars to parenthood. To violate this principle is to deliberately violate the fundamental laws of Nature, as well as those principles which are accepted as representing the best thought and customs of the race. A mental, moral or physical 'pervert' or 'defective' is manifestly 'unfit', considered as a prospective parent. Parenthood on the part of such individuals is not only a crime against society, but always a base injustice perpetrated upon the offspring.

Some families have a 'bad family history' for inebriety; others for epilepsy; others for licentiousness; others for dishonesty—the history extending over several generations and including a marked number of individuals in each generation. Individuals of such a family should refrain from bearing children. The child has a right to be well born and to be protected from being brought into the world subjected to the handicap of a 'bad family history'. If individuals cannot endow their children with a good family history, they should refrain from bearing children—such is the Eugenic advice on the subject.

Preparing for Parenthood

A reasonable time of self-restraint and continence should be observed by the prospective parents before the conception of the child. This is borne out by the experience of the breeders of fine horses and cattle, who have discovered that the best offspring are produced when the animals have been restrained from sexual intercourse for a reasonable time; this precaution being particularly observed in the case of the male parent animal. It is claimed that Sir Isaac Newton was conceived after a period of over a year of total sexual abstinence on the part of his parents.

The minds of both parents should be exercised by reading the right kind of books, and by paying attention to natural objects of interest. The prospective parents should also develop and exercise their moral faculties in the period preceding conception. This course will tend to reproduce the same quality in the child. The reverse of this, alas, is also true. A case is cited of a man who procreated a child while plotting a nefarious crime; and the child in after life manifested a tendency toward theft, roguery and rascality, even at a very early age. The lack of moral fibre so often noticed in the sons of rich men who have attained their success through questionable methods is perhaps as much attributable to these pre-conceptual influences as to the 'spoiling' environment of the child after birth.

The actual time of the conception of the new life should be carefully chosen, so that it may occur under the best circumstances and conditions. The time chosen should be one in which a peaceful and happy state of mind is possessed by both parents. It is an awful crime to beget life carelessly and when in improper and unworthy mental states. Some people seem to think that the matter of begetting a child, like the matter of selecting a wife, should be left wholly to blind chance. Neither of these two important events can be too much safeguarded by wise and thoughtful consideration.

How to Improve the Race

In considering the question of improvement, it may be well to begin by taking some specific quality of an inheritable nature and examining its distribution among the population at large.

To take stature as an example. We have pigmy races of men and it is quite conceivable that some such race might deem it desirable to increase the general height of the population.

The people who are markedly above the average height will, in this case, constitute the desirable class; and those who are markedly under the average would be the undesirable. There is an intermediate class, the normal, which is many times greater than both of the others put together, constituting, indeed, the bulk of the population.

In the diagram overleaf the large square represents the enclosure completely filled with the people under consideration.

THE MAKE-UP OF THE HUMAN RACE

In the diagram the *desirable* and *undesirable* classes each constitute one per cent of the population and the *normal* 98 per cent. The desirable and undesirable classes are very small as compared with the normal.

If, then, they decide to marry, it is obvious that most of the desirable and undesirable individuals will marry normal persons, because normal people constitute the bulk of the community with whom they come into contact; and the offspring will tend to revert to the normal type of the race.

From this it follows that, on the whole, the offspring of the desirables will be less desirable than themselves; and the offspring of the undesirables more desirable; most of the offspring will be of the normal type.

The problem is how to increase the proportion of desirable children born from the normal population.

This can be accomplished by marriage with the members of the desirable class.

In the case considered, this would mean that persons of normal height would increase their liability to have tall children by marrying tall people.

Of course, it is only possible for a small proportion of the normal population to marry persons belonging to the desirable class, on account of limited numbers. The range of choice, however, may be extended by marriages with brothers or sisters or close blood relatives of desirable persons.

Success with Suckling

Women who have never suckled often experience difficulty in nursing on account of the sunken and flat condition of the nipples. The nipples may be drawn out by a common breast pump, by suction with a tobacco pipe, by the use of the hot-water bottle or by the application of a puppy.

Cold Baths are Best

> Maxim: *Frequent bathing is conducive to cleanliness; it imparts vigour to the muscles and nerves, and promotes alacrity and cheerfulness of mind.*

In a striking manner does the cold bath preserve and promote the health of the infant race. The cold bath is not only a serviceable application to children in health, but to those that are sickly also, especially the rickety.

It may be resorted to thrice a week. A sudden dip, twice repeated each time of using the bath, will be sufficient.

Immediately after bathing let the child be wrapped in a blanket and well dried, and if it be disposed to sleep allow it to do so; if not, it may be dressed and suffered to run about.

NB. Weakly children using the cold bath may wear a flannel shirt. The warm bath is rarely employed except in disease.

A Note on Tobacco and Children

Although eighty drops of the infusion of tobacco is a medium dose for a man of twenty years of age, remember that a boy of five, in general, cannot bear twenty drops without being sensibly more affected than the adult.

Many similar instances have also occurred in the course of my practice with regard to the administration of opiates to children and infants, especially the latter. It seems probable that children and infants require smaller doses than adults of all the more powerful narcotic medicines, such as opium, hemlock, foxglove, tobacco, woody nightshade, etc.

To Prevent an Outburst of Spirits

The humanitarian ideas, which are so much the fashion at the present time, have made magistrates unwilling to inflict the ancient method of correction, that of whipping. A boy under fourteen years of age may for certain offences be ordered to be birched. This is done by a police officer in private, though the parent may, if he so desire, be present.

A sharp punishment such as this is very often excellent, especially if the boy comes from a fairly respectable home, when his offence is very likely due to an outburst of spirits.

How to Amuse Children

We have no space in this small book to do more than touch on a few of the many interesting things boys and girls may do in these days. The following may, however, be of use in suggesting occupations.

Trussed Fowls

Comical encounters, which frequently take place on board ship between the boys, who are trussed by their elder shipmates, is called 'trussed fowls'.

Two boys, having seated themselves on the floor, are trussed by their playmates; that is to say, each boy has his wrists tied together with a handkerchief and his legs secured just above the ankles with another; his arms are then passed over his knees and a broomstick is pushed over one arm, under both knees, and out again over the other arm.

The 'trussed fowls' are now carried into the centre of the room and placed opposite each other, with their toes just touching. In the endeavour of each fowl, with the aid of his toes, to turn his antagonist over on his back or side, much fun is caused. The one who can succeed in doing this wins the game, but it frequently happens that both players turn over together, to the great amusement of those looking on.

Impressions with Sealing Wax

Impressions made with a pretty seal on sealing wax of different colours is a fascinating occupation, but not suitable for small children as there is danger of their burning their fingers with the lighted candle or match.

Cards in a Hat

Another impromptu amusement can be arranged with an old top hat and a pack of cards. The game is to stand the hat on the floor, stand about six feet off, and throw the cards into the hat one at a time. The boy or girl who gets the most cards into the hat wins the game.

Wayside Cribbage

This is a game for two players to be pursued either when taking a walk, or drive, or when travelling by rail. The game consists in each player looking out on her particular side of the road for the following objects: a ladder, wheelbarrow, pump, grindstone, drinking trough, white horse and a cat in a window, and for these the score is as follows:

For a ladder	5	For a grindstone	10
For a wheelbarrow	5	For a drinking trough	10
For a pump	5	For a white horse	10

and for a cat in a window, game.

The one who first scores 50 wins the game and a cat in a window is considered to bring the score up to 50 at any point.

Family Coach

This is a suitable game for a large party of young children, say from six to twelve years of age, with one of the elder ones to take the lead. Each child assumes the name of some part of a family coach, the coachman, the horses, various parts of the harness, the door, the window, cushions, door handles, step, spokes, axle, etc., etc. Then the leader improvises a story relative to a family coach, e.g.: How the family set out in it to pay a Christmas visit, giving elaborate details of the start, also describing an accident which occurred by the way, and as each

part is named which the children have chosen, the particular child representing that part must jump up from her seat, spin round and sit down again, and when the coach is named they all do so. A good narrator keeps the whole party on the qui vive and highly delighted, for as long as he can tell an amusing story; we have seen a large party spellbound for fifteen minutes.

Dolls

Dolls are a source of delight to almost all girls and even to some little boys, and it is wonderful how childish imagination endows these bags of sawdust with every charm and all the humanity which the child can comprehend. Doll nursing awakens feelings of tenderness, solicitude and motherliness, and there must be something radically wrong in the disposition of a little girl who does not care for a doll.

Games: A Word of Caution

Young people enjoy being together and making a cheerful noise and merriment, and it is quite right and natural that they should; but they must remember that what is fit for children is not becoming for girls and boys when they grow older. For instance, 'Hunt the Slipper' and 'Kiss in the Ring' are only fit for quite little children, who may romp about and be as friendly and intimate with each other as they please, without much harm. But when girls get into their teens they should learn to keep themselves more to themselves and not allow any familiarities, especially from boys or men.

Boys have marbles and trap-bat and cricket and games of their own, which they should play by themselves; and girls had much better keep to their own games, too, especially if they want—as they certainly also do—good rousing games to exercise their legs and arms and lungs.

Very pretty games with songs are now being taught in schools, and besides hoops and skipping and battledore and shuttlecock, which are capital girls' games, there are pretty dances, such as the Swedish dance, Sir Roger de Coverley, country dances, reels or ribbon dances, which they can play at or dance, either by themselves or with the boys, if they beg to come too.

The ribbon dances, which can be danced with strips of coloured calico if ribbon is too expensive, are particularly suitable, because, besides looking pretty, it gives every one something to do with their hands and prevents romping.

➤ Wise Words for Explorers ⬅ And Excursionists Alike

A French Revolution in Fast Food

They manage a great many things in France, especially regarding the convenience of travellers, better than we do in this country. I discovered a noteworthy instance on one railway at least, namely that running between Paris and Cologne, in which the 'Five minutes for refreshments' nuisance—or more properly, swindle—is done away with.

In the cafés on that road the dishes, cups, saucers, tumblers, in fact, all the table utensils are made of paper, so prepared by an insoluble coating to resist the action of heated viands and liquors. These are sold to the hurried traveller with the condiments, so that if he purchases a steaming cup of coffee or a cooling glass of ice-water he takes the glass or cup and saucer with him into the carriage and enjoys its contents at his leisure. The same if he selects cooked meats, vegetables, soup or other articles of food.

Furthermore, having enjoyed his meal comfortably in his seat in the carriage, he may throw the dishes from the window with as little regret as he would the stump of a cigar.

How to Visit an Old English Inn

The real old solid English inn is one of the grandest institutions which this country has ever produced. It still persists fairly prevalently, heaven be praised. It is emphatically a local show, and everybody and everything has been there for years, including the furniture, which is old-fashioned, comfortable and faintly shabby. The food is abundant, varied, English and gloriously cooked, and mostly comes from their own farm and kitchen-garden; if they had a tin-opener they have probably lost it. The shrewd, unassuming proprietor instals lavatory basins and gas-stoves in the bedrooms because he believes in comfort, but generally knows 'the old is better'. The staff is small and unobtrusive, but absolutely capable and on the spot when you want it. The tariff is regular and extras few. The water is always boiling, and if you take twenty baths a day it has nothing to do with the bill. The motherly head-waitress is ready with your special bay-window table, and your favourite dishes and particular cuts appear unobtrusively before you. She tells you items of local gossip because she knows you will be amused, and asks after all the friends who have ever come there.

In an inn of this kind, you will always be sure of a friendly welcome in the bar, whether it be the 'Gentlemen's Smoke-Room' or the public tap. In the former, with its comfortable if dilapidated Victorian armchairs, hard-backed Windsors and hunting trophies and prints, you may find an agreeable 'session' in progress between a group of farmers and local gentry, which will provide you with a wealth of interesting sidelights on crops, sport and local manners and morals, often with an individualistic political dash. Everyone welcomes you with a 'Good morning' and speeds you with a 'Good night'.

In the taproom you are in more crowded quarters, and must be careful not to get in the line of fire of a game of darts, or unwittingly occupy the seat of a local patriarch. The landlord (or 'gaffer') will be mingling in the general conversation at the bar, which, for all its sprinkling of profanities, will have a healthy, humorous tang, and will provide an object-lesson in the local dialect. Of course, some counties are friendlier to strangers than others, and if (though the chance is rare) you find that your presence in the taproom is creating an awkward pause, you should seize the first suitable opportunity to transfer yourself to the smoke-room.

How to Become a Blood-Brother

It was as I was leaving Yakoma that I first saw the ceremony of blood-brotherhood. A little chief insisted on becoming my blood-brother, and, anxious to see how it was done, I consented. The rite was carried out in the following manner: In the open air, and in the presence of all the assembled chiefs and people, I was seated opposite to my prospective brother. A small incision was made in each of our forearms, half-way between the hand and elbow, from which a little blood oozed. The proper performance would have been for each of us to lick the blood of the other, but on this occasion we decided to dispense with that part of the rite, merely rubbing the cuts one against the other, and thus commingling our blood. When this was done the representative of my 'brother' got up and began to beat two pieces of metal together—a knife and a gun-barrel, I think they happened to be—keeping up a monotonous tink, tink, tink, and talking to me as he did so. He recited a sort of commination service, somewhat to the following effect: 'If you ever make war on me, if you ever steal from me, if you ever wound me, etc., etc., may you die!' This is a good opportunity for him in case he may want to get anything from you, so his incantation often contains such threats as, 'If you do not give me plenty of guns, may you die!' After this, a similar performance was gone through by my representative, whose business it was to nullify my new brother's subtle demands. Finally the compact was sealed by an exchange of small presents.

This custom is not by any means a local one, but is found among nearly all the tribes that inhabit the districts of Central Africa. Stanley submitted to the operation often enough to have reason to complain that his arm became quite sore from the effects of these frequent incisions.

How to Rough It

Roughing it has various meanings and the phrase is oftentimes ludicrously mistaken by many individuals. A friend thought he was roughing it daily for the space of three weeks because he was obliged to lunch on cold chicken and un-iced champagne, and when it rained he was forced to seek shelter inside some very inelegant hotels.

To rough it, in the best sense of that term, is to lie down every night with the ground for a mattress, a bundle of faggots for a pillow and the stars for a coverlet. To sleep in a tent is semi-luxury and tainted with too much effeminacy to suit the ardour of a first-rate 'Rough'.

The traveller who has never slept in the woods has missed an enjoyable sensation. A clump of trees makes a fine leafy post-bedstead and to awake in the morning amid a grove of sheltering nodding oaks is lung-inspiring. It was the good thought of a wanderer to say, 'The forest is the poor man's jacket.' Napoleon had a high opinion of the bivouac style of life and on the score of health gave it the preference over tent-sleeping.

The only objection to outdoor slumber is dampness; but it is easy to protect oneself in wet weather from the unhealthy ground by boughs or India-rubber blankets.

One of the great precautions requisite for a tramp is to provide against thirst. Want of water overtakes the traveller sometimes in the most annoying manner and it is well to know how to fight off the dry fiend. All who rough it should drink well before starting in the morning and drink nothing all day till the halt. Keep the lips shut as much as possible. A good authority recommends a pebble or leaf to be held in the mouth.

Spirituous liquors are no help in roughing it. On the contrary, they invite sunstroke and various other unpleasant visitors incident to the life of a traveller. Habitual brandy-drinkers give out sooner than cold-water men and we have seen fainting red noses by the score succumb to the weather when boys addicted to water would crow like chanticleer through a long storm of sleet and snow on the freezing Alps.

How to Become an Alpinist

To begin with, not everyone can become an alpinist. Only those of a robust constitution and a heart which works well should undertake such violent exertion. And if one has a tendency to dizziness he had better confine his ascents to peaks frequented by cows. The beginner, however, one physically and mentally fit, should start with simple walks, keeping to mule paths until he gets accustomed to heights and precipices. When one begins to feel at home here he may try the goat paths, or undertake, with guides, small excursions somewhat more ambitious. One of the cardinal rules of mountain-climbing, however, is never to go alone, and this applies even to those following mule trails.

Upon arrival in one of the large alpine centres such as Zermatt, Grindelwald or Chamonix, the novice would do well to purchase at once a suit made of loden, or similar cloth, which is warm, waterproof, and strong enough not to tear on the rocks. Such clothes may be found ready-made almost anywhere in Switzerland for 50 or 60 francs, or made to order for 10 francs more. If one wants style, prices, naturally, are higher. Most tourists, nowadays, and many guides, wear short trousers, on the theory that they allow freer use of the limbs. Personally I prefer the old-fashioned long trousers and spiral puttees, as I find in both snow and rocks that the legs are better protected.

Perhaps more important than clothes are a good pair of mountain boots. These may be purchased before starting, or on the spot, for about 35 francs, but should be bought sufficiently large to admit two pairs of woollen socks, a light and heavy pair. It is advisable to have the boots nailed in the alpine centres, as the bootmakers there know better than anyone else how to do this.

With a suit of loden, nailed boots and a large rucksack the beginner is ready to commence training. With an alpenstock costing one franc, or, better yet, an ice-axe costing about 15 francs, he may begin with walks lasting two or three hours, gradually lengthening his walks without, however, bringing on great fatigue. As one grows accustomed to the rarefied air and the muscles become supple, all-day walks may be undertaken, for it is not difficult to find good mule trails going up seven or eight thousand feet. It is very important in ascending that the stride be even, the entire foot solidly placed on the ground, and the pace at the start very slow. The reason for this is that the heart must adjust itself gradually to the violent strain, and if one goes rapidly at first, stopping frequently to catch breath, the adjustment does not take place. As a rule, if the heart begins racing, the climber may feel sure he is going too fast.

It is an ordinary sight in the mountains to see trained alpinists outstripped by tourists in a great hurry, who smile with derision at the tortoise pace of the former; but if one could see the picture higher up, the alpinists, who rarely stop, would be seen gradually increasing their speed, while the tourists would be lying on the grass holding their stomachs or leaning against a tree and breathing like a blown cab horse.

Just what the equipment of an alpinist should consist of is a question difficult to decide. A quart Thermos bottle, which will keep coffee or tea hot indefinitely, comes very near being

a necessity, for a cup of hot tea at a high altitude may be taken at a critical moment when the stomach refuses all other nourishment.

Some guides carry up a great deal of wine, which is a bad habit and sometimes becomes dangerous. Dr Hunter Workman, the celebrated Himalayan explorer, told me that while crossing a difficult passage in the Tyrol his guide was taken with the delirium tremens. It was his turn, therefore, to become guide, and they got down only after the greatest difficulty. After long experience he has found that it is better not to drink any alcohol in making an ascent, but afterwards a little whisky taken in a cup of tea aids in relieving the stiffness of the muscles. Not long ago I made a climb in the Mont Blanc range, starting with a young man who insisted on drinking a glass of absinthe. He was quite accustomed to this glass down in the valley, but it made him ill and consequently he had to abandon his climb.

There is no finer exercise than mountain-climbing. Ascensions are made in an atmosphere absolutely pure and in sunlight unknown in the valleys. On the summits one meets with unexpected panoramas of marvellous splendour, which have a healthy influence on one's ideas. And besides the ever-changing vistas there is the pleasure of struggling with the mountain, often menacing and sometimes fatal. It is in struggling with the forces of Nature that the individual develops courage, energy, sang-froid, prudence, decision and initiative. The mountain, therefore, is a great educator.

How to Speak Arabic

At first all the letters look alike; but, when once that difficulty is mastered, it is easier to get on. The pronunciation of the gutturals is quite dreadful and my teacher tells me that there are thirty-five different ways of forming the plural; but the words are so expressive that they are not difficult to remember.

The most useful Arabic words are: *Emshi ruh*, 'Go away'; *Mush auz*, 'I don't want it'; *Kettir khayrak*, 'Much obliged'; *taib*, good; *mush taib*, bad; *la*, no; *Neharak saida*, 'Good morning'; *Liltak saida*, 'Good night'; and a few *mashallahs, bismillahs* and *inshallahs* can be thrown in at discretion. The Arabic numerals, up to ten, are very handy in making purchases. *Bukra fil mishmish* is an invaluable joke with which to get rid of an importunate crowd. It means, I believe, that you will distribute 'green apricots tomorrow', and is received with unfailing delight.

Native Pipe-Smoking

Everything is used on the Congo for making a pipe that can possibly suggest itself, such as antelope horns, ivory, calabashes. To make a pipe out of a calabash, however large it may be, holes are bored at the two ends. In one is fixed a little clay cone, which serves as a bowl, and the smoke is drawn through the other end of the fruit without any stem. These pipes, when they belong to a negro of quality, are decorated

with brass-headed nails. When an antelope horn is used for smoking purposes, the wide end is applied to the mouth, and the operation of smoking through one of these is more productive of energy than of elegance.

The natives do not smoke their pipes through; that would be too laborious and painful an operation. As a rule the chief lights the tobacco at a glowing brazier, takes a few puffs, and the pipe is then passed round the circle in order of precedence. The consequent spectacle is amusing. The man whose turn it is to take a draw is eager to lose none of his rights; with surprising vigour he expands his lungs to their greatest extent, and fills his nose and eyes with the powerful fumes, which make him cough till the tears run down his cheeks, as his neighbour holds out both hands anxious to lose none of his share. While all this takes place with ceremonious formality, the smoking party seem as serious as if they were celebrating some mysterious rites, so that the impassiveness of their faces adds to the absurdity of the scene.

Rules for Motorists

Above all, have mercy upon timid women, dogs and little children.

If you have no imagination you will have no idea of the horrors of apprehension suffered by many a woman alone in a pony trap who sees your approach and does not know whether you mean to stop or not. If she makes a sign, hold up your hand to show that you have seen it and go past her (it may not be necessary to stop) as quietly as possible.

The only thing you need have little mercy on is the unattended horse dozing in the empty village street. Frighten him, if you like, and chivvy him far away from the place of inattention; he is a scourge and a danger and people who have to pay for many sets of broken harness will soon learn not to leave horses unattended.

If you are threatened by a dog, go slowly; he may be a senseless, ill-conditioned, barking cur, but he has a right to his life; and besides, you may be seriously hurt yourself if you run over him.

As for children, you had better go very gingerly in their neighbourhood.

In a little while a new generation of children will grow up wary of motor-cars and trained, poor mites, in the taking of cover; but in the meantime remember that the bit of village street through which you flash on your hundred-mile journey is their life and contains for them all the sunshine, all the dangers, all the pleasures and toil of life.

Motor Hooliganism

There are those in whom the intoxication that springs from the control of power and speed has bred the motor hooligan.

Remember, you were once perhaps capable of enjoying a quiet walk on a country road and that you did not always own a motor-car.

Remember that if you whoop through a village some Sunday morning in the summertime and meet a crowd of decent villagers going to church, the clouds of dust that you raise may spoil their Sunday clothes, fill their mouths with grit and their hearts with bitterness!

How to Behave on a Sinking Ship

'Be prepared' is as good a motto for the steamship passenger as for our Boy Scouts, for when on the sea danger or disaster may come at any time. It may be that a fog will be encountered, and the fast or heavy vessel crossing the track of your ship is not seen until too late. Or it may be that icebergs or rocks are about, which prove very unkind to sea-going vessels. Therefore the passenger should always be ready to turn out of his or her cabin directly called upon to do so, and make their way, without fuss or 'losing their head', to the weather deck. Before leaving their cabins, passengers should see that the porthole is closed, as every hole in the ship's side will probably count either as a direct cause of the loss of the ship, or as to the length of time the vessel may remain afloat.

Be sure that you get up to the weather deck as speedily as possible, as it may be necessary for the safety of the ship to close certain hatches on the weather deck, and the hatch leading to your cabin may be among them.

Do not go on deck in response to an emergency call without taking your lifebelt with you. Your neglect to do so will probably cost a brave man his life in surrendering his own lifebelt to you, so that you may be among the saved.

If you find any of your fellow-passengers 'losing their heads', do your best to bring them into line, so that perfect order and discipline is able to be maintained.

If it is necessary to take to the boats, do so in an orderly manner, and under the direction of the ship's officers, and do not forget the British rule, 'Women and children first', if you please.

Introducing the Occult to the Curious

Automatic Writing for Beginners

To become an automatic writing medium it is necessary to sit at a table with a pencil and some notepaper. Hold the pencil as if about to write; a feeling of numbness or trembling will come over the hand, the pencil will begin to move and in a short time you will be able to write and answer questions that may be put to you, either mentally or in sealed packets by persons that you may sit for.

To develop this power may take a few weeks. Some persons develop sooner than others. It is best to sit about twice a week.

Everything should be quiet and the mind kept passive. In some instances the spirit communicating will give information on various points, places and things that are altogether unknown to the medium. It is an invaluable means of ascertaining whether one's relatives, friends or acquaintances in foreign parts are well or ill.

The writing may not be very good at first, but it improves as the medium develops. Some mediums can write beautiful poetry and in some cases music, when under control. Handel, the great composer, wrote the *Messiah* while under control.

I have seen persons that could not read or write when in the natural state; but when they have practised automatic writing, have in a very short time been able to write short sentences and answer various questions. Sometimes the writing has been hard to decipher, but it has been found to be correct, although the spelling has been faulty.

Ghosts in Photographs

Most photographers during the development of their plates occasionally have what are called 'fogged plates'. They do not

expend much time, if any, in attempting to ascertain the cause
of the fog. But, while developing packet after packet of excellent plates, one or more is cloudy, the image is not clear and
in some cases not discernible at all. In these cases the busy
photographer has no time to waste: he writes for his customer
to give him another sitting and the plate-maker is anathema-
tised for turning out bad ones.

Let us throw some light on these irregular productions.

Should a human form appear in the mist, no matter how
indistinct, we advise that the photographer should communi-
cate privately with his customer, ascertain if such a form was
or is known to them and act accordingly. For it is possible that
unseen operators may be at work on the plate, endeavouring
to prove to their loved ones that they are risen and are taking
an intelligent active interest in all that concerns those from
whom death has apparently severed them.

Many professional photographers get clearly defined forms
on their plates, forms who have not stood in the studio before
the camera, in the body. They break up these plates immediately, for fear the fact should get about and damage their
connection.

However, positive science recognises a vital or psychic aura
surrounding inorganic life, although comparatively few people
have a luminous aura. This explains why when spirits are
photographed there are so few taken that are clearly defined.
Certain protective conditions are necessary to retain this
luminosity in its greatest purity and brilliance, which the
world at present does not recognise.

Nevertheless, the revelation of Psychic Photography has
caused a rumbling in the ground upon which the materialist
rested—a rumbling prophetic and indicative of the earth-
quake shock which is destined to overthrow all the deductions
of material science!

How to Cultivate a Magnetic Gaze

To cultivate a magnetic gaze hang a looking-glass on the wall about five feet from the floor. Get a small piece of white paper about the size of a shilling and gum it in the middle of the looking-glass. Then sit in a chair in an easy position opposite the glass, about four feet away. Fix both eyes on the piece of white paper. Stare at it for about five minutes at a time. Don't blink much, the eyes will water at first, but that will soon be overcome. Practise the above about three times a week till proficient. Do not think about anything else; only look at the paper and keep your mind clear.

The cultivation of a magnetic gaze is very important, as by its power things can be seen in a clearer manner and a person's mind better understood. A lion has a good gaze, as also have a cat and a hawk, but man has the best gaze of any animal on this planet.

Travellers in Africa and India have been known to turn away with fear lions, tigers, etc., when by fixing upon them their eyes, trained by gazing at various objects, and in times of peril have been able to save their lives. Had they lost their gaze it would have meant sudden death. You will have noticed how lion-tamers in menageries, etc., keep their eyes fixed on the animals with which they are performing.

A cat, by fixing its eyes upon a bird, a mouse or rat, can overpower them. Similar fascinating powers are found in the snakes in which it is enabled to charm a bird from the top of a tree and make it come down and devour it. A spider can also do the same thing with the fly, but the spider has its web to help it.

Boxers, fencers, etc., in gymnasiums have the gaze highly developed, and when they are engaged at an assault-at-arms they keep their eyes fixed on their opponents. It is a strange thing that they don't look at their opponents' hands or swords; they simply keep their eyes steadily fixed on each other, so that they can detect every movement.

In hypnotism it is essential to have a good gaze, so as to be able to influence the subject and therefore put him to sleep.

The Ancients cultivated the gaze by looking into rivers and staring at the Sun, Moon and planets.

So you see it is a most important thing to develop a good gaze. Concentrate the mind on any object you like and you will be surprised to see how your power will increase for doing good.

How to Read a Crystal Ball

When you have cultivated the gaze, you may get a crystal ball, put it on the table and put black velvet behind it, so that nothing in the room will reflect in it. You should fix it and look at it towards the north, as a northern light is the best.

Everybody has not the gift for crystal gazing, but most people have, if they will persevere; but it is like learning any other art or science, it takes time to get to perfection.

It is best to look into the crystal ball at regular times, about two or three times a week, till you get proficient, then you may look through for your friends. At first you will be able to perceive small images of persons, sometimes faces, that you will be able to recognise; also seawater, ships, wedding or funeral scenes, trees, fields, hills, animals, various kinds of buildings, money, papers, documents, railway trains, accidents, shining stars and pictures of various things.

It is best to look through the crystal ball for someone who is in serious trouble, so you can get better results, because the client's mind is properly concentrated on the business he wants to know about. In that case the client should hold the crystal ball between both hands for about five minutes; everything should be quiet. Then put the crystal ball on the table and after you have gazed at it, describe what you see. Some people experience a trembling feeling in their hands and arms, and sometimes it goes through their body. That is a good sign. It shows that their human magnetism is affecting the crystal ball and as a rule very good results are obtained.

Different individuals affect the crystal ball in different ways; sometimes it looks very dark, black, gloomy and cloudy. That is a very bad sign, which shows trouble, sickness, enemies, death, etc. Other times it looks very bright and silvery. That is a good sign, which denotes success and prosperity. A coffin denotes a death. Bright silvery stars are very good. To see money is a good omen; also property. Trains denote journeys; ships and seawater, voyages. Wedding parties are good. When the crystal ball looks a milky colour, it shows that things are in a very unsettled state for the client. You must always speak what you see, whether it is good or bad, for by so doing you might be able to warn your client and save him a great deal of expense and trouble.

Some very wonderful things are accomplished at the present time by crystal gazers. When you have acquired the gift of crystal gazing your services will be much sought after by all classes of people and the good you will be able to do will quite eclipse your expectations, for it will be a pleasure to yourself and a benefit to humanity.

How to be a Clairvoyante

To become a clairvoyante, rest on a couch or an easy chair. When in a recumbent position close the eyes and let the mind remain blank. Then fix the mind on some object or place you wish to see. You will be surprised to find how well you will be able to see things mentally. Then in time, when you learn how to go under control, you will have guides and they will show you things; and you will see objects that you have never seen before when in the natural state.

It is necessary to practise about twice a week. Evening is the best time. The sitting should last about an hour. The room ought to be made rather warm to start with; about 60 degrees Fahrenheit will do.

When you are able to go under control you will be able to see the spirits around people, spirits of children, women and men; also bright lights, gold and silver balls, scenes of various places, musical instruments, flowers, etc. When going under control do not be afraid, because if you are you will not see as much as you ought to do. Some mediums can go under control at will; others when in bed; some when ill.

It is not absolutely necessary to go under control to see clairvoyantly. Some can see spirits walking about in the day-time and also funeral coaches before a certain door, ere the person is dead.

Clairvoyantes have been known to find hidden treasure and lost stolen property. They have also been able to describe thieves, murderers, etc.

By following the above rules for development you will soon make rapid progress towards becoming a truthful and scientific clairvoyante and you will be much sought after by people who are in deep trouble, and therefore you will be able to do a great amount of good to suffering humanity.

Familiar Spirits

'Seek unto them that have familiar spirits, and unto
wizards that peep and that mutter.'

Isaiah 8:19

When the pact with the Devil has been struck it is not
unusual that there should be assigned to the witch a familiar,
that is to say an attendant demon or mysterious entity to obey
the behests and serve in various bad ways the pleasure of the
witch. The familiar or Astral spirit who companions with and
carries out the directions of the witch is a demon—it may be
of the higher orders, it may be of some lower grade. We find
that the more hardened and resolute in evil is the witch, the
more powerful and malignant, and therefore we may suppose
the higher in rank is the familiar.

These beings are often invisible to any save the witch
and often they exhibit themselves in human or animal form
and are plainly manifest to everyone. It does not need any
psychic perception to see them. Almost invariably their dark
supernatural origin can be recognised by some hideously
grotesque feature or deformity and even when such blemish
is hidden they carry with them an effluvium of evil which
betrays them to the horrified spectator. It is seldom that
the familiar can altogether conceal the features, blasted and
seared by Divine Wrath, of the fallen angel, but such cases
have been known.

Familiars are employed by the witch for purposes of divina-
tion and also for various hurtings and harms, for mischief
generally, to destroy property, to afflict with illness, to

raise jars,
Jealousies, strifes, and heart-burning disagreements
Like a thick scurf o'er life.*

* Lines from *The Witch* (1609–16), a play by Thomas Middleton (1580–
1627). [Ed.]

In his *Institute of the Laws of Scotland*, Edinburgh, 1722–1730, William Forbes writes that 'to some [the Devil] gives certain Spirits or Imps to correspond with, and serve them as their Familiars, known to them by some odd names, to which they answer when called.'

At Oxford, not much more than ten years ago, one of the best-known figures in the University was commonly believed to entertain a familiar. The presumption seemed borne out by some curious facts and happenings. Myself, I never saw plainly any strange corporeal form going to and fro with the wizard—for wizard he undoubtedly was—but on several occasions in brilliant sunshine as he walked the streets there moved at his side a dark and quite distinct man's shadow other than his own, a shadow which could not possibly have been cast by any person in his proximity, and, what is more, if he happened to pass certain churches—for example, St Aloysius or Blackfriars—this shadow would vanish completely away.

A Summary of Your Mental Powers

*Once the palmist has read your palm, he or she will present you with this card, having marked the paragraphs relevant to you.**

1. You have inherited a very inferior nature and will not think for yourself. You are low and vulgar in your habits.

2. You do things and believe in things because others do, seldom exercising your judgement in any matter. You look with wonder at talented individuals. Remember you are a human being and be more ambitious and try to elevate yourself.

3. You have a moderate degree of intellect and you will be appreciated by most persons, more especially by your employers, provided you keep steady. Be careful, though, lest they have an undue influence over you. Stick to one pursuit and be willing to learn and you will be more successful in life.

4. You possess an average intellectual organisation and if cultivated would be able to accomplish much. Look away from customs and fashions and make up your mind to succeed.

5. You have good reasoning powers and will not take for granted what you are told by others, but you think for yourself. You like science and literature and new thoughts and plans are constantly coming before you. If you carry out one quarter of your ideas you will do sufficient for a lifetime and your abilities if put to proper uses ought to enable you to make a mark in the world.

6. You are possessed of that which is God-like—'intellect'. You are a deep reasoner and have great refinement of mind. You test everything before believing and will make your mark in the world.

---

* *Notice to Clients*: It must be thoroughly understood that what is given from palmistry does not teach that the events must absolutely occur, but that they probably will unless steps are taken to prevent their occurrence.

⊰ In Time of War ⊱

Handling Self-Abuse in Wartime

It is inevitable that during war self-abuse should increase enormously. This increase is to be expected. Wherever conditions arise favouring or compelling the segregation of large numbers of young men, there is bound to be an extension of the practice of self-abuse. This is lamentable, but it is true. And the same thing applies in regard to the opposite sex. Self-abuse is prevalent among the women who are physically or psychically segregated. It is far more common among women than among girls. It is, I fancy, far more common among grown women than among grown men.

As regards girls, there has never been the same public reaction to the problem as there has with boys. For one thing, the public does not associate self-abuse with females. And yet it is extremely common. For another thing, even where any such association is made, the vice is credited with producing nothing in the way of evil results. Probably this is because, in the case of the female, there is no possibility of self-abuse interfering with the capacity for performing the sex act, while in the case of the male it is credited with being a major cause of impotence.

Self-abuse can be overcome by the exercise of will power and perseverance, and the development of a healthy outlook on life. The problem of handling the evil of self-abuse in wartime is the problem of providing the youth of the country with opportunities for indulging in pastimes, recreations and hobbies. During the long winter months especially is there danger of the evil developing.

How to Stalk Your Neighbour

Stalk your neighbour in such a way that you want to be successful because it would be embarrassing for your neighbour to see what you are doing. When you are stalking an actual enemy, you will do your job as well as you can because you don't want to be killed. Of course, the perfect example of this sort of exercise would be the small boy stalking the schoolmaster with the risk of considerable punishment if he fails. At least try stalking someone who would not perhaps see the point of the joke if he saw you.

Having chosen your intended victim, keep your body perfectly balanced, with your rifle ready in a split second to be put in a firing position. Fix your eyes on the victim or on the point from which you may most easily kill him, and glide along with your eyes [*sic*] straining at every sound, breathing regularly in time with your footsteps, your fingers feeling the trigger, your mind prepared in an instant to freeze up so that you may listen better or because your victim is looking in your direction or has stopped his work or other occupation and is obviously listening.

In this way move to the killing position, as close as you possibly can to the victim without giving yourself away. Pause, and with equal care make your getaway.

You will find that the more anxious you really are that your victim should not notice your behaviour, the easier you will find it to do the job well.

How to Put a Bomb in a Post Office

You are now ready to place a bomb through a window of the post office which is being used by Nazi troops who are for the time being in occupation of your piece of the countryside.

How will you set about it? What is the proper way to practise for this?

Try first of all on your own, that is, without co-operation or consultation with other members of your unit.

Choose a time when quite a number of the neighbours, including the local policeman, are about. Don't mind if the local policeman, seeing you, gives chase. It will give you all the more opportunity of practice. And if he catches you and demands an explanation, it will be easy for you to give one.

Begin doing the right things as early as possible in the exercise, that is to say, get yourself on the alert at the earliest possible stage of the proceedings. Once you have put yourself on the alert, banish everything from your mind except the job in hand.

Here is an example of what you will not do. You will not get up from the table and say to your wife: 'I'm going into the back garden to fill a tin can with gravel off the path so as to put it on the post office window-sill.'

Don't do this, not so much because your wife may think the worst of you unless you waste a great deal of time in explanation, but because you would not tell your wife if you were going on such a hazardous expedition.

To begin with, you would not start from your own house. You would not keep the bomb in your own house. You would have a secret rendezvous from which you would start.

Very well, do the same now. Keep your tin can in the wood a

mile away. Start your stalk from that wood. See to it that you have got the right equipment and nothing else.

If you have time, strip yourself right down to your under-clothes, and then say to yourself: 'My job is to put this bomb on the post office window-sill. What should I wear?'

Put nothing on that will not be valuable for the job. You will need your tunic and trousers quite certainly. You will need your socks, but will you need your boots? Wouldn't your job be better done in a pair of dark gym shoes?

Will you need your rifle? A rifle in the dark may possibly be used to kill somebody at about five yards' distance, but you are not out to kill anybody, and a rifle in the dark is a clumsy, difficult thing to manipulate. Probably if you think the thing over carefully, you will leave your rifle at home.

If you are heard, somebody may shine a light on you. You therefore see to it that your face and your hands are covered with green blanco.

If you want any arm at all, the probability is that a grenade in your pocket will be the best thing for you to have. You might have a chance of throwing it in a useful direction.

In this way you clothe and arm yourself wisely, but not only that. Everything that you decide to do has been thought out with a view to doing the job in hand. Although the job is only a practice, an exercise, the mere fact of this makes it real. You will feel yourself to be a hunting animal, you will not spoil everything by your frame of mind.

If, on the other hand, you do things halfheartedly, if you don't think about your equipment, if you don't green your face, if you do tell the family at the supper-table, you will sim-ply be a self-conscious civilised human being engaged in doing something which seems stupid and hoping to heaven that none of your neighbours will catch you at it.

When you have put your bomb on the post office window-sill, decide in your mind how long you are going to time the fuse. Give it ten minutes. Glide away in the darkness to a suitable spot. Sit there with your eyes on your watch, and when the ten minutes have passed say to yourself: 'There goes the post office.'

Even then, your exercise is not at an end. The post office has been blown up, the Germans are scouring the streets to find victims, hostages. They will certainly choose a man like yourself if they find him with a green face.

Hurry back to your home, maintaining every precaution, get into the house without your wife knowing it, wash your face and slip into bed without waking her. She will then be in a position to swear, if interrogated in the morning, that her husband was in bed at the time the explosion took place.

I have often said before, and I repeat again, that the Home Guard or modern soldier who does not know how to get into bed with his wife at 3 a.m. without his wife being kept in ignorance of the fact that he has been out of the house at all is not sufficiently well-trained to do his job against German invaders.

French for the Front

Privates learn twice as fast when they start French in rhyme. I have therefore written a series of short French verses for them and trust they may prove of real benefit to all Servicemen.

Nous sommes anglais	We are English
Nous sommes tous prêts	We are ready
A combattre les Allemands	To fight the Germans
Toute la journée.	All day long.
Etes-vous bien sûr	Are you quite sure
Que cette eau soit pure?	That this water is pure?
Est-elle empoisonée?	Is it poisoned?
Pouvons-nous l'employer	Can we use it for the tea?
pour le thé?	

Les boches	The Germans
Sont là!	Are there!
Couchez-vous	Lie down,
Ne parlez-pas!	Don't speak!
Touché	Hit
Au doigt!	In the finger!
Bandez-le	Bandage it
Pour moi.	For me.
Main	Hand
Cassée!	Broken!
Echarpe,	Sling,
S'il vous plaît!	Please!
Jambe	Leg
Cassée!	Broken!
Planchette	Splint
S'il vous plaît!	Please!
Sang	Blood
Perdu?	Lost?
Oui	Yes
Monsieur!	Sir!
Vue	Sight
Perdue!	Gone!
Soignez	See to
Mes yeux!	My eyes!
Mon capitaine est blessé,	My captain is wounded,
Mes camarades aussi;	My comrades too;
Apportez donc un brancard	Bring a stretcher
Et mettez-les à l'abri.	And put them under cover.

LIFE SKILLS GUARANTEED
TO FETCH OUT THE CAPACITIES
AND ABILITIES OF PERSONS
OF QUALITY

How to be Amused

All healthy people like to be amused and in every home there ought to be facilities for obtaining pleasant indoor recreation for the long winter evenings. In these days one need not lay out a lot of money or go very far to find ample aids to amusement.

Billiards is an unfailing source of pleasure and no finer indoor game has ever been invented, though many ardent devotees of chess and cards will doubtless be found to argue the point.

There are, of course, innumerable other pastimes which are adopted for the household. Draughts is always popular and there are a host of more modern games of all descriptions which cost little and give endless delight. A few of these should be on hand to promote cheerfulness during the dull days and long nights, when time seems to drag and ordinary occupations and recreations, such as needlework, music and reading begin to pall.

Whatever it may be, a man or woman, boy and girl, should make a point of selecting some healthy amusement which will quicken the sense of perception, improve the mind and the physique and promote social intercourse. In this way their own lives will be made all the happier and they will bring sunshine into the lives of others.

How to Smile

Here is a mighty good way to *start* a SMILE: Look into your mirror—smile at YOURSELF—let your mind and thoughts dwell on the most pleasant subjects imaginable.

Use all the might and force within you to provoke a smile if necessary—then watch it grow. If you don't believe it possible, just try it—do so NOW—are you doing it? I'll bet that you are SMILING already. Yes, and your smile will soon break into a laugh. That's it—now keep it up—take one good, long look at yourself in the mirror—one laugh ripples into another, and the provoking smile has long since vanished—isn't it easy?

If you've started the effort in the proper spirit you are already wearing the 'SMILE THAT WON'T COME OFF!'

If for any reason you haven't as yet mastered the situation, just try this: Make a real GROUCHY face—just as grouchy and disagreeable as you know how—don't be afraid that you will get it too grouchy, because you CAN'T to suit the purpose in hand. After you have accomplished this, if it be at all possible, just keep it up for a while—now look into your mirror again—does it not tell a pitiful story—isn't it AWFUL?

Now try a SMILE! It will even come more readily—the contrast is greater and more marked. You can now see the difference more clearly than you could before—why the very fact that you are ABLE to make that horrible grouchy face has been enough to make you laugh in itself.

This done—now make a resolution to SMILE under any and all circumstances. You can soon learn to do it without the mirror, for it will come most natural. Everyone will smile with you, for, as the old, true, but trite saying runs, 'LAUGH, AND THE WORLD LAUGHS WITH YOU; CRY, AND YOU CRY ALONE!'

Try provoking a smile on the next person you meet—the grouchier they are the better—say something pleasant and smile—notice the change of expression on the one against which your efforts are aimed.

Get a hold of the very worst grouch you ever knew—the woman or man possessed of the most sordid nature—start your prospect SMILING—you certainly can if you stick to it long enough. TRY EVERYTHING—be witty—be agreeable—radiate the sunshine of your nature right into their being through the means of a subtle smile. You can, if you want to—if you will only TRY. Your efforts will surely be rewarded by seeing them SMILE IN SPITE OF THEMSELVES.

Carry a little pocket mirror with you—show the grouches their own faces in this mirror—show them how much NICER they would look with a smile—resort to anything in order to provoke it—even though you have to tickle them. Once the glimmer of a smile is reflected back on to them they will HAVE to take it up and expand it in spite of themselves. Needless to say your grouch-friend will be much better off for the experience.

Your little pocket mirror should be your boon companion. Perhaps you only THINK you're smiling when you're not. Maybe the smile indulged in isn't the right sort of smile after all—perhaps it is forced or faint-hearted. In that case you'll know the truth by consulting your little mirror.

Practise this little seeming idiosyncrasy on the sly, by yourself, away from the gaze of others—do not let anyone get the idea that VANITY prompts you to look at yourself so much in the mirror. YOU know what you are doing and you know why you are doing it, so that's enough.

Keep right at it and you will soon have that 'HABITUAL SMILE' which is so much coveted by all those who are harassed with woes and worries.

How to Shoot a Giraffe

These animals are very difficult of approach for they are extremely keen-sighted and their towering height enables them to command a wide view. When several are together, as is generally the case, they are especially hard to stalk, since it becomes impossible to keep out of sight of all those different pairs of eyes up among the tree-tops. It is then only by the most careful, painstaking stalk, exercising every precaution, regardless of sun, thorns and other inconveniences, and very likely spending a long time over it, that the hunter can hope to arrive within shot.

The modern small-bore rifles are most effective on this, as on most, if not all, kinds of game. The heart or lungs may be reached from any position and a shot there is very quickly fatal. It is necessary, though, to be particularly careful not to aim too high, as the immense width of the base of the neck tends to deceive the eye as to the position of the vitals. If the neck is the only part of the giraffe visible, a shot in the centre of the neck will break the spine and drop the animal on the spot.

Suddenly the tall dappled form

staggers, sways and then falls crashing to the earth. Another bullet ends its struggles. The hunter, streaming with perspiration, surveys with keen interest the wonderful prize stretched out before him and lights a welcome pipe. Presently his bushmen spoorers come running up, hot upon the trail. They have a long and tough business of skinning before them and for the next hour or two the hunter and his assistants have plenty of employment in dismantling and cutting up their quarry.

Improving Your Memory

There are two ways of curing the worst memory. One of them is to read a subject when interested; the other is to not only read, but think. When you have read a paragraph or a page, stop, close the book and try to remember the ideas on the page. Do not only call them vaguely to mind, but put them in words and speak them out. Faithfully follow these two rules and you have the golden keys of knowledge.

Besides inattentive reading, there are other things injurious to the memory. One is the habit of skimming over newspapers, items of news, smart remarks, bits of information, political reflections, fashion notes, so that all is a confused jumble, never to be thought of again, thus diligently cultivating a habit of careless reading hard to break. Another is the reading of trashy novels.

How to Cultivate the Body

Many people think that a gymnasium is a place for sporting men. This is a mistake. Clergymen, physicians, students, clerks, governesses and society people frequent respectable gymnasiums. The gymnasium of today is a very different place from that of fifty years ago. Formerly the aim of gymnastics was to turn out men who could lift heavy weights and court death on the flying trapeze. Nowadays all this is changed. Physical training is carried on in a scientific manner; men of ability have made physical culture a profession and their object is to make pupils healthy, strong and graceful. Most modern gymnasiums have appliances for the cultivation of every part of the body, and able instructors and physicians in attendance.

I advise all young and middle-aged men and women to spend an hour daily in earnest systematic physical exercise. The best plan is to enter a gymnasium where some system is employed. There are several systems of training: the Swedish, the German, the English and the so-called American system, which is just a mixture of the German and Swedish. The Swedish and the German systems are considered by competent judges to be the best.

The German system embraces three departments: school gymnastics, popular gymnastics and military gymnastics. The aim was to make the youth of Prussia strong and courageous to defend their country when needed.

The Swedish version is a system of voluntary movements arranged and executed with care: leg movements, back and chest movements, heave movements, shoulder movements, respiratory movements, balance movements, abdominal exercises, etc.

The English system of free athletic exercises has been tried with great success in France. No doubt it has a wonderful influence on the moral and social qualities of the young.

How to Smoke

As a brain soother which enables men to bear with more equanimity the ills of life, whether mental or physical, tobacco has no equal. Smoking in moderation is certainly not injurious, and may have a very beneficial effect upon the health by allaying nervous irritation and checking a tendency to worry. It also promotes social intercourse among men in a wonderful way, which is to be counted among its greatest virtues; but to the lover of tobacco, a pipe, a cigar, or even the ubiquitous cigarette, is a congenial companion in itself, and with it he will seldom feel lonely.

A prime cigar is a true luxury, but for general smoking nothing beats a good briar pipe charged with a really choice mixture—one of those scientific blends which have been evolved by a manufacturer who really knows that tobacco is something more than a noxious weed to be destroyed by slow combustion in a clay tube. There is an endless variety of tobaccos to choose from, and every taste is catered for, but the perfect 'smoke' is rare and must be sought for like diamonds and radium.

An ideal tobacco should be pleasing to the palate, cool, and possessing a pleasant aroma when burning and an agreeable smell when in the pouch. The strength will depend upon individual taste, and it is hardly necessary to say that no one should persist in smoking a tobacco which produces a feeling of nausea; though, as a matter of fact, some beginners do keep on trying to accustom themselves and their stomachs to a tobacco strong and rank enough to make a seasoned veteran sick.

How to Perform an Emergency Baptism

I suppose you know that when a child or grown-up person is in danger of death and is unbaptised, anyone may baptise— yes, anyone; a layman, a woman—anyone who has himself been baptised may baptise another in exceptional circumstances. Two things alone are necessary: water and the name of the Holy Trinity. You will find the words in the service of Private Baptism in the Prayer-book.

Be very particular about both if you are called upon to baptise.

Don't sprinkle water, pour out of the palm of your hand a

little water; let there be no doubt about the water: not on the face, but on the head, because that is much more convenient and does not make the child cry.

Also pour a little water *three times*, once with the name of each person of the Holy Trinity. If it is very cold weather warm the water. The form is: '*I baptise thee in the Name of the Father and of the Son and of the Holy Ghost. Amen.*'

But don't sign with the cross. This is done by the clergyman when at length he comes and receives that child or person 'into the Church' with the appropriate words.

Be careful also to *put down on paper* all you have done: the way you have used the water and the name in which you have baptised.

How to Defend Yourself against a Mad Dog

A dog that is mad runs along snapping at everybody in his path. Every scout should know what to do when there is a mad dog about and should be prepared to do it.

The way to prevent a dog biting you is to hold a stick or even a handkerchief in your two hands across your front. The dog will generally try to paw it down before he actually bites you and you may thus get a chance of landing him a kick under the jaw.

On Hanging Considered as One of the Fine Arts

Where *all* authors have failed hitherto in their treatment of hanging is that they have never for a moment considered it as a fine art. They have not considered all that goes towards making a good job of it. They have omitted to mention a thousand and one aspects of the subject of interest to the moral philosopher and also of interest to all who are in any way concerned with hanging, from the hemp-picker who collects the raw material for making the hangman's rope to the gravedigger who prepares the quick-limed resting-place of the man, woman or infant who is hanged.

Let us begin then by considering hanging as a fine art. We may almost assume that it is a fine art and not a base mechanical trade. Is not a man an artist who can painlessly and without brutality dispatch another man? There is a certain delicacy about the operation which needs a ready eye, a swift-working brain, cool and calculating, and a cleverness which is only to be found in the realm of the great arts. The architect constructs a great building from a significant series of outlines; the musician constructs an entire symphony from a single series of tones; but our hangman by one pull of the lever achieves far more than either.

The beauty of hanging is recognised by its effects on the mind, just as the beauty of a Velasquez painting is recognised in the same way; and we must be content to leave it at that. Benedetto Croce calls art *intuition*. Who among us cannot immediately recognise *by intuition* that hanging is an art and the executioner an artist? Hanging has all the characteristics of art: conservatism, the elaboration of an instinctive mode of expression, balance, harmony in effects, rhythm, tone; and effect.

The office of hangman has never yet received its due either in praise or in rewards from the British public. A mere baker's dozen of human beings is executed by us every year and the English hangman could never hope merely by virtue of his office to become a rich man.* Although this may be in the best tradition of the Government Service, you will agree that it is deplorable. And it is all the more deplorable when we compare the delicate art of the hangman with that of the 'electrocutioner' or the guillotiner or the garotter of other countries less civilised than ourselves. What skill is required to turn a switch? What skill is required to twist a garotte? What skill is required to decapitate with the aid of an elaborate engine? I

* He is paid £10 for each person he kills; the perquisites are no longer great.

do not include in the same category as these three the German method of beheading with a sword. Thank Heaven there is still some art—or rather science—remaining on the Continent of Europe. The Germans go even further than we do in recognition of their science, for their executioner performs his ceremony in full evening dress, like a violinist playing a symphony to an enraptured audience at the Wigmore Hall.

But to return to the vexed question of art. Before a man is hanged the hangman has to assume the parts of a mathematician, a scientist, an engineer and an expert in dynamics. Combined with these he must have the mind of a philosopher and the soul of one who practises art for art's sake. This must be so, because he is so badly paid that nothing but the subconscious drive which impels great artists towards their major achievement could otherwise account for his choice of this greatly underestimated and somewhat unrespected profession.

Having measured the man to be hanged, taken his weight, examined the contours of his neck (and felt its muscles), the hangman who has a job of work on hand must next see that his apparatus is in good working order. If he omits to oil his lever and bolts and also the hinges of the trap-door upon which his subject is to stand, he may easily bungle the whole thing.

The Perfect Public Hanging

The actual hanging process could be made extremely impressive if executions were held in public. To do full justice to the ceremony, it would be necessary to employ an *impresario* and then the State could reap considerable financial benefits from public executions.

There are round about London many admirable open spaces suitable for the execution of criminals. Shambles could be appointed in convenient parts of the metropolis, say in Hyde Park, Regent's Park, Trafalgar Square and on the Horse Guards Parade for the special convenience of members of the

Cabinet and their families, who from rooms in No. 10 Downing Street, the Foreign Office, the Treasury, etc., would be provided with a good view and be able to contemplate the hangman at work. Binoculars would bring it all still closer.

The massed bands of the Brigade of Guards could discourse sweet music and the archbishop of Canterbury, or his deputy on less important occasions, could preach a sermon based upon the text '*An eye for an eye, a tooth for a tooth*', or they could vary this with '*Who so sheddeth man's blood, by man shall his blood be shed; for in the image of God made He man.*' The pipers of the Scots Guards could no doubt add to the sermon a suitable lament, for the benefit of the assembled populace.

The prime minister would be able to see the hangman put the finishing touches to his victim, see him pause to glance to see that all is ready; the pull of the lever, the sickening fall, the crack of doom and the last paroxysms of the body.

The jury who found the prisoner guilty could afterwards file up to shake hands with the executioner and congratulate him upon his proficiency. A special gallery conveniently situated should be provided for the British Medical Association and the Council should be present with stop-watches. As a final wind-up, the archbishop of Canterbury or his deputy should say the Lord's Prayer, emphasising the words *Thy will be done on earth as it is in Heaven*. By way of further variety, an eminent official theologian of the modernist brand should make a speech showing that Christ was mistaken in His whole idea of redemption and that the Sermon on the Mount does not stand the test of higher criticism.

A Ready Reckoner for Hangmen

RULE—Take the weight of the Client in Stones and look down the column of weights until you reach the figures nearest to 24 cwt., and the figure in the left-hand column will be the DROP.

Distance falling in feet. Zero.	8 Stone			9 Stone			10 Stone			11 Stone			12 Stone			13 Stone			14 Stone			15 Stone			16 Stone			17 Stone			18 Stone			19 Stone		
	cwt.	qr.	lb	cwt.	qr.	lb	cwt.	qr.	lb	cwt.	qr.	lb	cwt.	qr.	lb	cwt.	qr.	lb	cwt.	qr.	lb	cwt.	qr.	lb	cwt.	qr.	lb	cwt.	qr.	lb	cwt.	qr.	lb	cwt.	qr.	lb
1 ft.	8	0	0	9	0	0	10	0	0	11	0	0	12	0	0	13	0	0	14	0	0	15	0	0	16	0	0	17	0	0	18	0	0	19	0	0
2 ft.	11	1	15	12	2	23	14	0	14	15	2	4	16	3	22	18	1	12	19	3	2	21	0	21	22	2	11	24	0	1	25	1	19	26	3	9
3 ft.	13	3	16	15	2	15	17	1	14	19	0	12	20	3	11	22	2	9	24	1	8	26	0	7	27	3	5	29	2	4	31	1	2	33	0	1
4 ft.	16	0	0	18	0	0	20	0	0	22	0	0	24	0	0	26	0	0	28	0	0	30	0	0	32	0	0	34	0	0	36	0	0	40	0	0
5 ft.	17	2	11	19	3	5	22	0	0	24	0	22	26	1	16	28	2	11	30	3	5	33	0	0	35	0	22	37	0	16	39	2	11	41	3	15
6 ft.	19	2	11	22	0	5	24	2	0	26	3	22	29	1	16	31	3	11	34	1	5	36	3	0	39	0	22	41	2	16	44	0	11	46	2	5
7 ft.	21	0	22	23	3	11	26	2	0	29	0	16	31	3	5	34	1	22	37	0	11	39	3	0	42	1	16	45	0	5	47	2	22	50	1	11
8 ft.	22	2	22	25	2	4	28	1	14	31	0	23	34	0	5	36	3	15	39	2	25	42	2	7	45	1	16	48	0	26	51	0	8	53	3	18
9 ft.	24	0	11	27	0	12	30	0	14	33	0	23	36	0	16	39	0	18	42	0	19	45	0	21	48	0	22	51	0	23	54	0	25	57	0	26
10ft.	25	1	5	28	1	23	31	2	14	34	3	4	37	3	22	41	0	12	44	1	2	47	1	21	50	2	11	53	3	1	56	3	19	60	0	9

Hints for Hiring Servants in the Colonies

The supervision of native servants is an art in itself, and one in which the qualities which make success or failure seem ingrained. One could not, for instance, learn by experience in England when is the right time to have a servant beaten for rubbing silver plate on the gravel path to clean it, and that after several previous warnings.

Having arrived up country, about the first operation will be to collect one's staff of servants. Native servants will be found very fairly good, and soon assimilate any knowledge that one is in a position to impart. Unfortunately, as they learn the virtues of English domestics, they attain the drawbacks of the same with equal celerity. They have been known to sample the whiskey or to retire beneath the floor of the house with a full jam pot, there to lie *perdu* until it is empty; and a course of training will enable them to vie with any parlour-maid in crockery smashing.

How to Take a Strong Man Prisoner Single-Handed

Threaten him with your gun and compel him to throw his arms away; then, marching him before you some little distance, make him lie flat on his face and put his hands behind him. Of course he will be in a dreadful fright, and require reassuring. Next take your knife, put it between your teeth, and, standing over him, take the caps off your gun, and lay it down by your side. Then handcuff him, in whatever way you best can. The reason for setting to work in this way is, that a quick supple savage, while you are fumbling with your strings and bothered with a loaded gun, might easily spring round, seize hold of it and quite turn the tables against you. But if the gun had no caps on it would be of little use in his hands, except as a club; and also, if you had a knife between your teeth, it would be impossible for him to free himself by struggling, without exposing himself to a thrust from it.

To tie a man's hands behind his back, take a handkerchief, it is the best thing; failing that, a thin cord. It is necessary that its length should not be less than 2 feet, but 2 feet 6 inches is the right length; for a *double* tie, it should be 3 feet 6 inches. Wrapping the cord once (or twice if it be long enough) round the arms, press tightly, pass the longest end in between the arms and tie quite tightly. If you are quick in tying the common 'tom-fool's knot', well known to every sailor, it is still better for the purpose. Put the prisoner's hands one within each loop, then draw tightly the running ends, and knot them together. To secure a prisoner with the least amount of string, tie his thumbs together.

How to Execute a Legitimate 'Rabbit–Killer' Punch

There is one stroke used in boxing that is very effective, but one rarely sees it done. I refer to the back of the neck punch on a man who rushes in with his head down. Here your opponent has usually hurled himself at you crouching low and sent a punch at your body. This you sidestep; then, turning instantly and keeping very close, bang down a punch on the back of his neck as he flies past. The blow is not the illegitimate 'rabbit-killer' (i.e. a downward chop with the side of the hand), but a perfectly fair punch, delivered with the full knuckles of the hand.

Delivered powerfully, the stroke is probably the most difficult move in the whole art of boxing; not only must it be done with great quickness, but one has to keep so close to one's opponent when sidestepping as to be almost touching him. Jim Driscoll* is the only boxer I have seen make a complete success of the move. In the last fight he had before retiring, he used the punch repeatedly, not only after sidestepping to the right, but (more difficult still) after sidestepping to the left. Nothing is a better criterion of a boxer's skill than to be able to work this stroke properly, both to left and right, and amongst the present-day boxers I know of no one who is capable of using it on a good opponent; indeed, many of our first-class boxers do not even appear to know of its possibility.

* 'Peerless' Jim Driscoll (1880–1925), British, Empire and European Featherweight Champion. [Ed.]

How to Treat a Hysteric

Nervous people, especially women, get hysterics when excited, crying, laughing and screaming. The best treatment is to shut the patient into a room and leave him entirely alone till he gets over it. Don't try and soothe him, it only makes him worse.

How to Stop a Runaway Horse

Accidents are continually occurring from runaway horses running over people. In fact, on an average, the number of runaway horses that are stopped by policemen during the year amounts to over two hundred; and it is well that everybody should know how to stop a runaway horse.

The way to stop a runaway horse is not to run out in front of it and wave your arms, as so many people do, but to try and race alongside it, catch hold of the shaft to keep yourself from falling, seize the reins with the other hand and drag the horse's head round towards you, so turning him until you can bring him up against a wall or house or otherwise compel him to stop.

How to Tell an Imbecile from an Idiot

Insanity so closely resembles vice in some forms that it is sometimes a difficult matter to distinguish when a person is actually insane. There are many different forms of insanity.

An imbecile is one who is mentally defective from birth, but who has the power of speech; while an idiot is the same, but unable to speak. Another form is lunacy, which cannot be mistaken and is unsoundness of mind occurring in a person whose mind is fully developed previously.

It is often difficult to detect insanity, especially in the case of a person whose mental balance is disturbed in one direction only. This particular form is called mono-mania. For instance, a person may be talking quite sensibly with a mono-maniac for some time and on mentioning a certain person or article he commences to rave about them.

No attempt should be made to deceive a lunatic, as the loss of his confidence means the loss of the power of control over him. A doctor should be engaged to examine the state of the mind of anyone who is suspected of insanity in any form and if the case is unsafe, immediate removal to an asylum will be necessary.

Suicide for Scouts

Where a man has gone so far as to attempt suicide, a Scout should know what to do with him.

In the case of a man cutting his throat, the great point is to stop the bleeding from the artery, if it be cut. The artery runs from where the collarbone and breastbone join up to the corner of the jaw and the way to stop bleeding is to press hard with the thumb on the side of the wound nearest to the heart. Pressure should be kept up as hard as possible until assistance arrives.

In a case where the would-be suicide has taken poison, give milk and make him vomit, which is done by tickling the inside of the throat with the finger or a feather or pouring down his throat a tumbler of water mixed with a tablespoonful of mustard or salt.

In the case of hanging, cut down the body at once, taking

care to support it with one arm while cutting the cord. Cut the noose, loosen all tight clothing about the neck and chest. Let the patient have as much fresh air as possible, throw cold water on the face and chest or cold and hot water alternately. Perform artificial breathing, as in the case of apparently drowned people.

A tenderfoot is sometimes inclined to be timid about handling an insensible man or a dead man or even of seeing blood. Well, he won't be much use till he gets over such nonsense; the poor insensible fellow can't hurt him and he must force himself to catch hold of him; when once he has done this his fears will pass off. And if he visits a butcher's slaughter-house he will soon get accustomed to the sight of blood.

How to be a Ventriloquist

If the ventriloquist is a good performer, the voice appears to come from, say, the roof of the house. The secret of this art lies in practising what is called the ventriloquial drone.

Take a deep, long breath, which you must hold in your lungs and make a reaching sound at the back of the throat, as though you were trying to vomit. As you do so, make a sound like a low grunt, exhaling slowly at the same time. Do this several times.

Now instead of the grunt try to say the vowel 'ah'. When with a little practice this 'ah' settles down to a sustained clear hum like that of a distant bee drone, your success is assured.

When you can drone on the vowel 'ah', try 'eh' and so on through all the vowels. Do not attempt any words at present, but you may try 'bah', which will give the sound of distant sheep, and 'caw' for crows, etc.

Now stand before a looking-glass and speak a few easy words such as *oh*, *we*, *which*, etc., and endeavour, while in the act of speaking, to maintain a fixity of countenance so that no visible movement may be noticed in the muscles and nerves of the face and lips.

Practise thus for half an hour each day for a week; the actual duration of each exercise need not exceed ten minutes.

Next practise the vowel sounds *a e i o u* without disturbing that expression, proceeding to sound the consonants *d g k l n r s t* in the same manner. Then try *da, de, di, do, du* and so on for all the other consonants. Then try *ad, ed, id, od, ud; ag, eg, ig, og, ug,* etc.

The remaining consonants—*b, p, f, v* and *m*—cannot be pronounced without at least some slight movement of the face, to the great discredit of the ventriloquist, so it is necessary to omit them. Thus, for 'a very fine day', say 'a werry wine day'; for 'mind what you are about', say 'mind what you are awout', etc.

To perform successfully in public it is necessary to work on the imagination of the audience and thus bewilder them as to the direction from whence the sound proceeds.

Take your stand at one end of a large room, keeping far away from the audience. You may give a short speech in an easy and natural manner, then call out 'Hallo!' Repeat with force the answering 'Hallo!' Then proceed as follows:

VENTRILOQUIST (*looking up*): Hillo. Is anybody there?

VOICE: Hillo!

VENTRILOQUIST: Where on earth are you?

VOICE: Hillo! I'm here, up the chimney (say: *Ing here, uch the chigney*).

VENTRILOQUIST (*goes to chimney*): What are you doing there?

VOICE: I'm putting a clean collar on (*Ing hfuting a clean collar on*).

VENTRILOQUIST: A very strange place to put on a clean collar.

VOICE: Not at all; it is a very suitable place (*a very suitagle hclace*).

VENTRILOQUIST: Oh, no doubt, it's soot-able enough up there. Well, come down.

VOICE: All right. I be a-coming down.

VENTRILOQUIST: Are you here now?
VOICE: I'm here now.

The performer who understands his business will, of course, gradually increase the volume of the ventriloquial voice, not forgetting the acting—that is, at the last phrase, stoop down towards the mouth of the chimney and start back, as though surprised.

How to Seize Control of the Means of Production

If you do resolve upon a general taking over of the sources of wealth; if some fine day you wish to walk into the mines and factories and set the wheels going for the purpose of producing goods for your own use, instead of for your employer, nothing is surer than that you will be met by the powers of government and forbidden at the point of the bayonet to do so. If then you shall still believe that government is a necessary and a righteous thing, you will quietly retire with Christian submission and face your deepening, irremediable misery with the meek virtues of a slave. But if you see, as you should, that government is in that hour what it is now and always has been, in all its forms, an organisation of armed force for the purpose of perpetuating slavery and maintaining slave-holders in their possessions, then you will assert your right to be free men.

Short of this, you cannot be free people. If you so declare yourselves in the face of governmental force, you may win your freedom as slaves have won their freedom until now.

Whether the winning shall come dear or cheap will depend on how thoroughly the whole mass of the working people shall realise their condition and be penetrated with the desire for freedom. If the army, the militia and the police, composed in the main also of the poor, shall have been awakened to their own miserable situation, and have become sensible of the despicable 'service' that they do as the watchdogs of landlords, bankers and employers, then when the day of the declaration of social freedom dawns, great numbers will go over to you; it is even possible that the disintegration of governmental force may be such as to give you a bloodless victory. But peaceful or otherwise, that victory must be won before there can be plenty, security and liberty for man.

Fix your eyes on that and move directly towards that. Never listen to any siren song about winning the powers of government first; government will make of your representative what it has made of every one else in its service, its hireling, its time-server. Delegate no powers to anyone; take the earth and its wealth directly, yourselves, as soon as you are strong in will and unity.

How to Avoid Work

How many people are there who don't enjoy their jobs? All of my studies indicate that a decided majority are dissatisfied and wish they were doing something else. Imagine how much frustration all this vocational maladjustment is causing! No wonder so many people are irritable nowadays.

What about yourself? Is your job work or fun? If it is work, then you would probably be wise to take immediate steps to get out of it. Your life is too short and too valuable to fritter away in work.

As I walk into offices, through factories and stores, I often find myself looking into the expressionless faces of people going through mechanical motions. They are people whose minds are stunned and slowly dying.

When a person is in a job he dislikes, he reacts by being moody and nervous. He becomes tired easily and is a victim of indigestion and insomnia. As he continues to feel frustrated, he becomes rebellious, figuratively kicks at people, grows sour on the world. Yes, forcing yourself to work at a job you dislike is like wearing a lead vest to run a race—it's just plain exhausting.

Most people think that once you get started in a certain field, you can't very well change. This is sheer nonsense.

No matter who you are, what you've been doing, or how old you are, you can change to a job environment more agreeable to your nature. There is no such thing as a one-and-only career for anyone. Frequently there are several possible careers open to you that will be equally satisfying. It is only when you get caught in a job that is wholly alien to your nature that you develop ulcers and a nervous breakdown.

Life really begins when you have discovered that you can do anything you want.

To my mind, the world would be a much pleasanter and more civilised place to live in, if everyone resolved to pursue whatever is closest to his heart's desire. We would be more creative and our productivity would be vastly increased.

Altogether too much emphasis, I think, has been placed on what we *ought* to do, rather than what we *want* to do.

To some people, doing what you want to do seems almost sinful. But, believe me, it is not sinful. It is not selfish. It is not something a person should feel guilty about. If your life is important, why waste it in disagreeable work that has no meaning to you?

When we consider that each of us has only one life to live, isn't it rather tragic to find men and women, with brains capable of comprehending the stars and the planets, talking about the weather; men and women, with hands capable of creating works of art, using those hands only for routine tasks; men and women, capable of independent thought, using their minds as a bowling-green for popular ideas; men and women, capable of greatness, wallowing in mediocrity; men and women, capable of self-expression, slowly dying a mental death while they babble the confused monotone of the mob?

For you, life can be a succession of glorious adventures. Or it can be a monotonous bore.

Take your choice!

SOURCES

Every effort has been made to contact copyright holders; in the event of an omission or error, the editorial department should be notified at The Folio Society, 44 Eagle Street, London WC1R 4FS.

Excellent Remedies for Various Ailments

TO CURE THE TOOTHACHE: (1) Sidney Oldall Addy, *Household Tales with Other Traditional Remains*, 1895; (2) Lady 'Speranza' Wilde, *Ancient Legends, Mystic Charms and Superstitions of Ireland* (London: Ward & Downey, 1888); (3) *Journal of the Royal Institute, Cornwall*, 1915.

AVOIDING BITES AND STINGS, THE IMPORTANCE OF FRESH AIR: *The Family ABC, Containing Indispensable Advice for Every Home* (London: Simpkin, Marshall, Hamilton, Kent & Co., Ltd, 1911).

TWO CURES FOR BALDNESS: Bernard of Gordoun, *Lilium Medicinae*, 1305, cited in Patrick Logan, *Irish Folk Medicine* (Belfast: Appletree Press, 1999).

ARSENIC CURES: Thomas Fowler, *Medical Reports of the Effects of Arsenic in the Cure of Agues, Remitting Fevers and Periodic Headaches* (London: J. Johnson, 1786).

TO STOP BLEEDING: (1) Devon Hewett, 1900; (2) Orkney *Notes and Queries*, 1834; (4) John Aubrey, *Miscellanies*, 1696; (5) Lupton, 1579, all cited in *Penguin Guide to the Superstitions of Britain and Ireland*, ed. Steve Roud (London: Penguin Books, 2003); (3) Alice Thomas Ellis, *Fish, Flesh and Good Red Herring* (London: Virago, 2004). Reprinted by permission of Peters, Fraser and Dunlop and the Time Warner Book Group. © Alice Thomas Ellis 2004.

A WORD ABOUT GOUT: John Colbeck, *A Treatise of the Gout, Wherein both its Cause and Cure are demonstrably made to appear* (London: Daniel Brown, 1697).

THE MEDICINAL QUALITIES OF TOBACCO: *The Book of the Household or Family Dictionary of Everything Connected with Housekeeping and Domestic Medicine* (London: London Printing and Publishing Co., Ltd, n.d.).

A UNIVERSAL REMEDY: John D. Gimlette, *Malay Poisons and Charm Cures* (London: J. & A. Churchill, 1915).

THE WONDERS OF THE AIR-BATH: Revd. William Martin Trinder, *The English Olive-Tree or A Treatise on the Use of Oil and the Air-Bath* (London: S. Gosnell, 1812).

A PAINLESS METHOD FOR CURING PILES, A REMEDY FOR MELANCHOLY: Alexander Newton, *Piles: How to self-cure them without cutting, ligature, nitric acid or any painful process* (London: Henry Kimpton, 1887).

CURES FOR WHOOPING COUGH: *The Manufacturer and Builder*, Volume 6, Issue 3, March 1874 (New York: Western & Co., 1874).

THE PROPER USE OF THE WARM BATH: W. H. James, *Observations on the practical utility of the warm-water, medicated vapour, fumigating sulphur, cold shower and medicated baths in the cure of rheumatism, gout &c.* (London: Hampstead, 1830).

HOW TO CURE A MADMAN: William Mather, *The Young Man's Companion, or The Several Branches of Useful Learning Made Perfectly Easy* (London, 1761).

THE ALCOHOLIC CURED: *The Manufacturer and Builder*, Volume 8, Issue 4, April 1876 (New York: Western & Co., 1876).

A REMEDY FOR SLEEPLESSNESS: *The Manufacturer and Builder*, Volume 7, Issue 8, August 1875 (New York: Western & Co., 1875).

Essential Etiquette

THE MARKET VALUE OF GOOD MANNERS: H. E. Norton, *Courtesy: A Reader for Older Boys and Girls* (London: Macmillan & Co., Ltd, 1900).

THE IMPORTANCE OF CONFORMITY, ONIONS, ETC., WHEN TO MAKE AN INTRODUCTION, PULLING OUT ONE'S WATCH, GLOVES, STAIRS, ON THE STREET: *How to Behave: A Pocket Manual of Etiquette and Guide to Correct Personal Habits* (Glasgow: John S. Marr, 1867).

HOW TO CONVERSE IN SOCIETY, HOW TO CONVERSE WITH LADIES, A WORD ON POSTURE AND BEARING, HOW TO EAT: *How to Behave, or The Etiquette of Society* (London: Ward, Lock & Co., 1879).

THE CORRECT ARRANGEMENT OF THE MALE ORGANS: O. S. Fowler, *Creative and Sexual Science* (New Brunswick: Thompson & Company General Agents, 1876).

HOW TO HOST A DINNER PARTY: *The Family ABC, Containing Indispensable Advice for Every Home* (London: Simpkin, Marshall, Hamilton, Kent & Co., Ltd, 1911).

Delicious Recipes for Discerning Chefs

SUGAR MICE, TURTLE SOUP, BEAR RUMP ROAST, SEVENTEEN SQUIRRELS IN A POT, HOW TO COOK AND EAT A LIVE GOOSE: Alice Thomas Ellis, *Fish, Flesh and Good Red Herring* (London: Virago, 2004).

A HUNTER'S BREAKFAST: W. B. Lord and T. Baines, *Shifts and Expedients of Camp Life, Travel and Exploration* (London: Horace Cox, 1876).

RAW MEAT JUICE: *The Family ABC, Containing Indispensable Advice for Every Home* (London: Simpkin, Marshall, Hamilton, Kent & Co., Ltd, 1911).

BRAIN FRITTERS: *Daily Express War Time Cookery Book: Practical Advice and Recipes Specially Prepared for War Time Conditions* (London: Daily Express, 1940).

ROAST TONGUE AND UDDER: *The Book of the Household or Family Dictio-*

nary of Everything Connected with Housekeeping and Domestic Medicine (London: London Printing and Publishing Co., Ltd, n.d.).

HOW TO COOK A HIPPOPOTAMUS: *Great and Small Game of Africa: An Account of the Distribution, Habits and Natural History of the Sporting Mammals, with Personal Hunting Experiences* (London: Rowland Ward, Ltd, 1899).

CRUNCHY FROGS: A. W. Chase, *Dr Chase's Recipes, or Information for Everybody* (Ann Arbor: Chase, 1866).

Flawless Beauty Tips for Plain People

HOW TO STAY YOUNG: *The Manufacturer and Builder*, Volume 26, Issue 2, February 1894 (New York: Western & Co., 1894).

BATHING BEAUTIES, A WORD OF ADVICE REGARDING CORSETS, HOW TO STOP BLUSHING: *The Family ABC, Containing Indispensable Advice for Every Home* (London: Simpkin, Marshall, Hamilton, Kent & Co., Ltd, 1911).

WASHING THE HAIR: *The Girl's Own Annual*, Volume 27 (London, 1907).

TO REMOVE FRECKLES, BANISHING BLACK SPOTS, REMOVING TARTAR, FOR TIRED EYES, A WORD ABOUT CHINS: Mrs Humphrey ('Madge' of 'Truth'), *How to Be Pretty Though Plain* (London: James Bowden, 1899).

Advice of a Delicate Nature

CONTINENCE: Lord Baden-Powell of Gilwell, Chief Scout, *Scouting for Boys* (Oxford: Oxford University Press, 2005). Used by permission of OUP.

CONCERNING 'STRANGE WOMEN': Revd. Innes B. Wane, *What to Keep From and What to Keep: Friendly Advice to Young Fellows setting out in Life and to others who have already traversed part of the journey* (London: Charles Murray, 1914).

HOW TO CHOOSE A WIFE: 'ZETA', *How to Choose a Wife* (Peterborough: E. B. Sargeant, 1853).

A NOTE ABOUT 'POPPING' THE QUESTION, BUILDING UP YOUR WIFE'S BREASTS: O. S. Fowler, *Creative and Sexual Science* (New Brunswick: Thompson & Company General Agents, 1876).

HOW TO SPOIL A HUSBAND: *The Manufacturer and Builder*, Volume 1, Issue 6, June 1869 (New York: Western & Co., 1869).

Some Excellent Observations on the Duties of Parenthood

FITNESS FOR PARENTHOOD, PREPARING FOR PARENTHOOD: R. B. Armitage, *Sex Advice to Women: For Young Wives and those who Expect to be Married* (London: Advanced Thought Publishing, 1918).

HOW TO IMPROVE THE RACE: Alexander Graham Bell, 'How to Improve the Race' in *The Journal of Heredity*, Volume V, No. 1, January 1914 (Washington, DC: The American Genetic Association, 1914).

SUCCESS WITH SUCKLING: Geo. H. Napheys, *The Physical Life of Woman:*

Advice to the Maiden, Wife and Mother (Philadelphia: George Maclean, 1872).

COLD BATHS ARE BEST: *The Book of the Household or Family Dictionary of Everything Connected with Housekeeping and Domestic Medicine* (London: London Printing and Publishing Co., Ltd, n.d.).

A NOTE ON TOBACCO AND CHILDREN: Thomas Fowler, *Medical Reports of the Effects of Arsenic in the Cure of Agues, Remitting Fevers and Periodic Headaches* (London: J. Johnson, 1786).

TO PREVENT AN OUTBURST OF SPIRITS: Revd. H. S. Pelham, *The Training of a Working Boy* (London: Macmillan, 1914).

TRUSSED FOWLS: *People's Penny Popular Book of Parlour Games and Indoor Amusements* (London: J. Salisbury, 1894).

IMPRESSIONS WITH SEALING WAX, CARDS IN A HAT, WAYSIDE CRIBBAGE, FAMILY COACH, DOLLS: *How to Amuse the Children, or Holiday Fun for Fine and Wet Days* (London: Grant Richards, 1901).

GAMES: A WORD OF CAUTION: *A Few Words to Boys and Girls on the Care of Their Bodies* (London: Hatchards, 1882).

Wise Words for Explorers and Excursionists Alike

A FRENCH REVOLUTION IN FAST FOOD: *The Manufacturer and Builder*, Volume 2, Issue 9, September 1870 (New York: Western & Co., 1870).

HOW TO VISIT AN OLD ENGLISH INN: Harry Batsford, *How to See the Country* (London: B. T. Batsford Ltd., 1940).

HOW TO BECOME A BLOOD-BROTHER, NATIVE PIPE-SMOKING: Capt. Guy Burrows, *The Land of the Pigmies* (London: C. Arthur Pearson Ltd, 1898).

HOW TO ROUGH IT: *The Atlantic Monthly*, Volume 8, Issue 50, December 1861 (Boston: Atlantic Monthly Co., 1861).

HOW TO BECOME AN ALPINIST: Frederick Burlingham, *How to Become an Alpinist* (London: T. Werner Laurie Ltd., 1914).

HOW TO SPEAK ARABIC: 'From a Lady's Diary' (the Lady being an anonymous member of Taylor's party) in Isaac Taylor, *Leaves from an Egyptian Note-book* (London: Kegan Paul, Trench & Co., 1888).

RULES FOR MOTORISTS, MOTOR HOOLIGANISM: Lord Montagu, *The Art of Driving a Motor Car* (London, 1906).

HOW TO BEHAVE ON A SINKING SHIP: Charles V. A. Eley, *How to Save a Big Ship from Sinking, Even though Torpedoed* (London: Simpkin, Marshall, Hamilton, Kent & Co., Ltd., 1915).

Introducing the Occult to the Curious

AUTOMATIC WRITING FOR BEGINNERS: Alexander Verner, *Table Rapping and Automatic Writing* (Bolton: A. Verner, 1903).

GHOSTS IN PHOTOGRAPHS: Thomas Sloaney Wilmot, *Twenty Photographs of the Risen Dead* (London: Simpkin, Marshall, Hamilton, Kent & Co., Ltd, 1894).

HOW TO CULTIVATE A MAGNETIC GAZE, HOW TO READ A CRYSTAL BALL, HOW TO BE A CLAIRVOYANTE: Alexander Verner, *Clairvoyance and Crystal Gazing* (Bolton: J. Fearnsides & Sons, 'Free Press', 1902).

FAMILIAR SPIRITS: Montague Summers, *Witchcraft and Black Magic* (London: Rider & Co., Ltd., 1946).

A SUMMARY OF YOUR MENTAL POWERS: Palmistry chart published in Blackpool (Occult Book Depot, Promenade, Blackpool, n.d.).

In Time of War

HANDLING SELF-ABUSE IN WARTIME: George Ryley Scott, *Sex Problems and Dangers in War-Time: A Book of Practical Advice for Men and Women on the Fighting and Home Front* (London: T. Werner Laurie Ltd, 1940).

HOW TO STALK YOUR NEIGHBOUR, HOW TO PUT A BOMB IN A POST OFFICE: Major John Langdon-Davies, *How to Stalk: A Practical Manual for Home Guards* (London: John Murray & the Pilot Press Ltd, 1944).

FRENCH FOR THE FRONT: E. F. Harris, *French for the Front: A Short Cut to the French Language in Rhyme* (London: E. Marlborough & Co, 1916).

Life Skills Guaranteed to Fetch out the Capacities and Abilities of Persons of Quality

HOW TO BE AMUSED, HOW TO SMOKE, HOW TO TELL AN IMBECILE FROM AN IDIOT: *The Family ABC, Containing Indispensable Advice for Every Home* (London: Simpkin, Marshall, Hamilton, Kent & Co., Ltd, 1911).

HOW TO SMILE: J. C. P. Bode, *How to Be Happy Though All Goes Wrong* (London: L. N. Fowler & Co., 1914).

HOW TO SHOOT A GIRAFFE: *Great and Small Game of Africa: An Account of the Distribution, Habits and Natural History of the Sporting Mammals, with Personal Hunting Experiences* (London: Rowland Ward Ltd, 1899).

IMPROVING YOUR MEMORY: *The Manufacturer and Builder*, Volume 12, Issue 11, November 1880 (New York: Western & Co., 1880).

HOW TO CULTIVATE THE BODY: Wilton Tournier in *Lippincott's Magazine*, extracted in *The Manufacturer and Builder*, Volume 26, Issue 8, August 1894 (New York: Western and Company, 1894).

HOW TO PERFORM AN EMERGENCY BAPTISM: Bishop Montgomery, D.D., *Advice to Churchmen about to Emigrate* (London: Society for Promoting Christian Knowledge, 1910).

HOW TO DEFEND YOURSELF AGAINST A MAD DOG, HOW TO TREAT A HYSTERIC, HOW TO STOP A RUNAWAY HORSE, SUICIDE FOR SCOUTS: Lord Baden-Powell of Gilwell, Chief Scout, *Scouting for Boys* (Oxford: Oxford University Press, 2005). Used by permission of Oxford University Press.

ON HANGING CONSIDERED AS ONE OF THE FINE ARTS, THE PERFECT PUBLIC HANGING, A READY RECKONER FOR HANGMEN: Charles Duff, *A Handbook on Hanging: Being a short introduction to the fine art of Execution, and containing much useful information on Neck-Breaking, Throttling, Strangling, Asphyxiation, Decapitation and Electrocution; as well as Data and Wrinkles for Hangmen, an account of the late Mr Berry's method of Killing and his working list of Drops; to which is added a Hangman's Ready Reckoner and certain other items of interest; all very proper to be read and kept in every family* (London: The Cayme Press Limited, 1928).

HINTS FOR HIRING SERVANTS IN THE COLONIES: Lady Cranworth, in Lord Cranworth, *A Colony in the Making, or Sport and Profit in British East Africa* (London: Macmillan & Co., 1912).

HOW TO TAKE A STRONG MAN PRISONER SINGLE-HANDED: Francis Galton, *The Art of Travel or Shifts and Contrivances Available in Wild Countries* (London: John Murray, 1872).

HOW TO EXECUTE A LEGITIMATE 'RABBIT-KILLER' PUNCH: Norman Clark, *How to Box* (London: Methuen & Co. Ltd, 1931).

HOW TO BE A VENTRILOQUIST: *How to Become a Ventriloquist*, Professor Barter (London: Simpkin, Marshall, Hamilton, Kent & Co., Ltd., 1898).

HOW TO SEIZE CONTROL OF THE MEANS OF PRODUCTION: Anonymous, *How to End Panics: An Address to Poor People* (New York: Anarchist Federation of America, 1908).

HOW TO AVOID WORK: William J. Reilly, *How to Avoid Work* (Surrey: The World's Work (1913) Ltd., 1950).

Acknowledgements

I would like to thank Kit Shepherd at the Folio Society, whose idea this was, and for his ingenious index, and the late Montgomery 'Bunty' Burrows for his moving preface. My thanks go to Richard Jenkyns, Professor of Classics at Lady Margaret Hall, Oxford, for his invaluable advice and I am grateful to the staff at the Bodleian Library for their help and support. Most of all I would like to thank my wife, Ali, who greatly assisted me in the labour of completing this book. At the behest of my publishers I would also like to take this opportunity to stress the absolute inadvisability of following much of the advice contained within these pages. Readers would do well to keep in mind the old Danish proverb:

'He who builds to every man's advice will have a crooked house.'

INDEX

acid, hydrochloric, as tooth whitener, 37

air: exacerbation of gout, 5; fear of fresh, 13; lung-inspiring, 59, 62; miseries attributable to impure, 13

air-bathing, instructions for, 7–8

alcohol: craving for counter-acted by capsicum, 12; incompatible with outdoor life, 60, 62; inflammatory effect on piles of, 8; *see also* brandy; delirium tremens; gin

Alps, *see* mountaineering

ammonia, liquid, role of in skincare, 35

ankles, thick, inadvertent display of, 21

antelopes, employment of horns, 64

Arabic: dreadful gutturals of, 63; invaluable joke in, 63

arsenic, medicinal value of, 2–3

ash trees, sympathetic, 4

Baker, Sir Samuel White, mode of cooking hippopotamus, 29

baldness: and carbonised raven ointment, 2; and exhumation of mice, 2

balls, crystal, procedures for gazing into, 71–2

baptism, emergency, 89–90

bathing: advantages of warm bathing, 11; as aid to composure, 38; as cure for 'beastliness', 41; effects on insanity of, 11; promotion of the infant race through cold bathing, 51; regularity of prerequisite for beauty, 33

bears, garlic roasted rump of, 27–8

'beastliness': means of curing, 41; not manly, 40; *see also* self-abuse

billiards, unfailing source of pleasure from, 83

birching, private administration of, 52

blackheads, banishment of, 34–5

blankets, india-rubber, 59

blood-brotherhood, proper performance of, 58–9

blouses, desirability of, 36

blushing, self-inflicted, 38

books, trashy: dangerous to health and spirits, 40; injurious to memory, 87

borax: as bath salt, 33; and eradication of freckles, 34

Boy Scouts: encouraged to kick mad dogs, 90; encouragement of continence in, 40–1; means of overcoming squeamishness in, 100; and suicide, 99–100

boys: dolls a source of delight to, 54; excellent effects of birching on, 52; pinioning of by shipmates, 52; and ribbon dancing, 55; stalking of schoolmasters by, 78; suitable quantity of tobacco for, 51; toe-wrestling by, 53; *see also* Boy Scouts

brandy, and treatment of tired eyes, 38; weakness of imbibers at altitude, 60

breasts, influence of flattery upon, 46; *see also* nipples

British Medical Association, front-row seats recommended for at hangings, 93

British Medical Journal, views on female underwear, 36

Canterbury, Archbishop of, sermons of for public hangings, 93

capsicums, as cure for alcoholism, 12

carbonatjies, extemporised, 24

cats: dried skin of, and toothache, 1; value of in windows, 54

champagne, un-iced, 59

children: care required by parents in procreating good children, 47–8; correct dosage of arsenic for, 3; entertained by throwing cards, 53; fascinated by sealing wax, 53; impersonation of carriages, 54; method of baptising without upsetting, 90; morally and physically upstanding parents a right of, 47; particular susceptibility to narcotics, 51–2; promotion of alacrity and cheerfulness in by immersion, 51; spellbound for fifteen minutes, 54; suffered to run about, 51; wariness of motor-cars, 65; *see also* boys; girls

chins: development of well-formed, 38; deterioration of the will and, 39

clairvoyantes, truthful and scientific, 73

clergymen: discourtesy exhibited by young men towards, 18; popularity of gymnasiums with, 87

coagulation, methods of achieving, 3–4

coffee: as cause of flushing, 38; necessity of for alpinists, 61–2; unhurried enjoyment of, 53

conformity, and proper regard for feelings of others, 15–16

Congo region, enthusiasm for smoking in, 63–4

constipation: and bringing on of desire, 41; obstinate, 6

conversation: avoidance of unworthiness in, 18–19; preparations for, 16–17

corsets: construction of on scientific lines, 36–7; indispensability of, 35; injurious effects of, 36

crêpe, funeral-smelling, 46

cribbage, wayside, 53

Croce, Benedetto, and aesthetics of capital punishment, 91

curtseying, aerobic value of, 8

dancing, capital for girls, 55

dehydration, remedies for, 60

delirium tremens, dangers of while mountaineering, 62

Devil, the, pacts with, 74–5

dialects, healthy humorous tang of, 58

dinner parties, deadly foes of enjoyment at, 22

dogs: right to life of ill-conditioned, 65; mad, 90

dolls, childish fondness for, 54–5

Driscoll, 'Peerless' Jim, legitimate 'rabbit-killer' punch of, 97

drone, ventriloquial, 100

drunkards: confirmed, 12; graves of, 46

eggs: attractive power of hard-boiled, 12; superiority over soap, 33

electricity, colonic application of, 10; means of counter-acting depression, 10–11

elephants: suitability for *al fresco* breakfasts, 24–5; trunk of best eaten cold, 25

enemas, tobacco-smoke, 6

eructations, disagreeable, 17

Eugenics, cardinal principles of, 47; and desirability of tall people, 48–50

executions, *see* hanging

exercise: advisability of earnest and systematic, 88; of the arm as means of subduing urges, 41; as cure for blushing, 38; and discharge of perspiratory matter, 7–8; for girls, 55; impediment posed by braces during, 36; intellectual, as aid to the complexion, 32; venereal, 5

exposure, naked, *see* air-bathing

Forbes, Sir William, and legal status of familiars, 75

France: novelty of paper plates in, 56; moral influence of English athletic exercises upon, 88; servicemen's vocabulary for, 81–2

freckles, eradication of, 34

fritters, brain, 27

frogs: only legitimate way of cooking, 29–30; sweet, melancholy *ch-r-r-rk* of, 30

games: family coach, 54–5; good rousing, 55; involving hats, 53; promotion of cheerfulness by in winter, 83; trussed fowls, 52–3; wayside cribbage, 53–4

gaslight, allure of strange women by, 41

gas-works, smell of, 11

gaze, magnetic, importance of possessing, 70–1

geese, cooking alive, 30–1

Germans: antagonism against expressed in French, 81–2; development of patriotism through gymnastics, 88; formality of executioners, 92; suspicious of green-faced men, 81

gin, fresh mixed, as exfoliant, 35

giraffes: especially difficult to stalk, 86; means of despatching, 86–7

girls: dislike of dolls by unnatural, 55; 'Hunt the Slipper' perilous for, 55; not associated with self-abuse, 77; pretty dances for, 55

gloves, etiquette for, 20

gnats, aversion to vinegar of, 1

gout, as proof of intelligence, 5

governesses, penchant for gymnasiums of, 87

government, as means of oppressing masses, 102–3

gravies, greasy, 8

haddock, miraculous properties of, 1

haemorrhoids, as cause of gout, 6; *see also* piles

Handel, George Frederick, spiritual possession of, 68

handkerchiefs: as defence against mad dogs, 90; prisoners restrained by, 96

hanging: aid to calculating correct drop, 94; artistic characteristics of, 91; financial benefits of public hangings, 92; hangman's superiority over other executioners, 91–2; Horse Guards Parade recommended as convenient venue for, 92–3; methods of reviving after, 99–100; musical accompaniments to, 93; sensitivity of practitioners, 92; as source of employment, 90–1; and theology, 93

happiness, pursuit of, 103–4

head-waitresses, motherly, 57

hippopotami: flavour of, 28; sink when shot, 29; unfamiliarity with clothes, 28

hobbies: and melancholia, 10; as substitute for self-abuse, 77–8

horseradish, as deep cleanser, 34

horses, imitated by children, 54; motorists' duty to frighten unattended, 65; runaway, 98

humour, attainment of by artificial training, 16

hysteria, best ignored, 98

Illinois, childcare in, 11

inns, old: great English institution, 57; likelihood of friendly welcome in, 57–8; plumbing and, 57

insomnia: and unhappiness at work, 103; means of counter-acting, 12

J. B. Side-spring, the, 37

James II, King, heroic nosebleed of, 4

juice: fatty (chyle), 32; raw meat, 26

ladies: able to baptise in emergen-
cies, 88; ability to ruin men, 44–6;
apprehension at approaching
motorists of, 65; appropriate style
of converse with, 18–19; attainment of perfect figure by, 35–7;
attention to posture in presence of,
19; and stair-case etiquette, 20–1;
characteristics of necessary in
good wives, 43–4; disadvantage to
of shoulder-suspended dress, 36;
display of thick ankles by, 21;
methods of accosting, 21–2; offer of
gloved hands to ill-mannered, 20;
perfect example of Classical in
matters of hygiene, 33; prone to
hysteria when excited, 98; protection of unattended, 18; susceptibility of, 44; see also womanhood,
true

lions, mastery of by human stare,
70–1

loneliness, countered by tobacco, 89

Lower Umfuli river, haunt of hippopotami, 28

madness: danger of disabusing
lunatics, 99; mistakable for vice,
98; imbeciles distinct from idiots,
99; treatment by immersion of, 11

manliness: 'beastliness' irreconcil-
able with, 40–1; and defencelessness of dependent sex, 19;
development of on mountain-tops,
63; and inappropriate intimacy, 18;
lack of in rich men's heirs due to
pre-natal influences, 48; and piles,
9; of voice prerequisite for marital
success, 44

manners: market value of, 14–15; for
motorists, 65–6

marriage: avoidance of vulgar and
uncultivated women, 44; and cruel
and disgusting traits, 43; importance of good domestic qualities,
43; necessity of marrying females

of average appearance, 44; over-
eagerness of young men, 42; public
criticism as restraint against pre-
mature, 43; quarrelsome propensities and, 43; ruinous influence
of wife in, 44–6; and shrivelled
breasts, 46; as training ground
for resistance against foreign
invaders, 81

mastication, audible, 23

meat: effect on piles of, 8–9; juiced,
26; promiscuous use of, 5; see also
bears; elephants; frogs; geese;
hippopotami; mice; squirrels;
tongue; turtles; udders

melancholy, means of combating,
10–11

Messiah, and spirit writing, 68

mice: exhumation of, 2; medicinal
properties of dung, 4; bronchial
benefits when sugared, 24

Middleton, Thomas, authority on
witchcraft, 74

mines, coal, medicinal value of, 11

motorists, over-exuberance of, 65–6

mountaineering: adoption of tortoise
pace during, 61; ascent of Mont
Blanc sabotaged by absinthe, 62;
boots, large and hob-nailed, 61;
character-building qualities of, 63;
necessity of Thermoses, 61–2; and
spiral puttees, 61; and vertigo, 60;
wisdom of wearing shorts during,
60–1

mustard, and attempted suicide, 99

Napoleon I, Emperor of the French,
views on camping, 59

Nash, William, miracle cure of, 4

Nature: struggles with forces of, 63;
violation of the fundamental laws
of, 47

Nazis, and post offices, 79, 81

newspapers, detrimental to the memory, 87

Newton, Sir Isaac, conceived after

prolonged sexual abstinence, 48
nicknames, mistimed use of, 18
nipples, flat and sunken condition of, 51; *see also* breasts
noses: application of toads to, 3; correct method of drying, 34–5; and self-improvement, 38

oils, scented, as ward against insect attentions, 1
onions, raw: as cure for insomnia, 12; impoliteness and, 17
opiates, administration to children of, 52
organs, male, correct arrangement of, 20
Oxford, as haunt of wizards, 75

palmistry, acuteness of, 76
parenthood: continence essential precursor to, 47–8; development of moral faculties prior to, 48; as injustice perpetrated upon offspring, 47; as means of improving human race, 48–50; and overcoming impediments to breast-feeding, 51
particles, alkalious, 5
passions: complexions ravaged by, 32; necessity of exerting manly control over, 9, 38
people, old: coagulatory power of, 3; perspiratory matter of, 7
photography, psychic, 69
pictures, lewd, 40
piles, electrical treatment of, 8–9; *see also* haemorrhoids
pills, anti-bilious, 10
plantains, haemostatic juice of, 4
poison: Boy Scouts and, 99; sovereign remedy for, 7
police officers: and birching of boys, 52; and runaway horses, 98
porcupines, sea, 7
post offices, principles for attacking, 79–81

pottage, milk, role in mental health-care of, 11
presentations, promiscuous, 17
puppies, application of, 51
puttees, spiral, 61

ravens, roasted, 2
romping, precautions against, 55
roots, jungle (unidentified), 7
ropes, correct length of for securing prisoners, 96
Rumford, Sir Benjamin Thompson, Count, interesting essay by, 11

Salisbury, royal nosebleeds and, 4
salt, as soothing eyewash, 38
Scoffern, Dr John, stringent tartar control by, 37
Scots Guards, role of pipe band in public executions, 93
scoutmasters, and 'beastliness', 41
scouts, *see* Boy Scouts
self-abuse: explosion of in wartime, 77; increased prevalence of in winter, 78; lack of evil results among women, 77; *see also* 'beastliness'
Sermon on the Mount, the, and the higher criticism, 93
servants, colonial, penchant for jam of, 95
Shakespeare, William, misguided marital advice of, 43
Sheridan, Richard Brinsley, as intellectual gladiator, 16
ships: danger of open portholes to, 67; maintenance of order and discipline on sinking, 67
siestas, threat to health of, 5
smiles: provocation of in others, 85; self-inducement of, 84
soup, turtle, 26
spiders: curative sniffing of, 4; fascinating powers of, 71

spirits: assigned to witches, 74; communication of through photographs, 69; composition of *Messiah* by, 68; evidence for in Oxford, 75; faulty spelling of, 68; visibility of, 73

squirrels, stewed, 29

stalking: difficulty of with giraffes, 86; embarrassment of discovery during, 78

standing, habit of early acquired, 19

Stanley, Sir Henry Morton, sore arms of, 59

suicide, methods for foiling, 99–100

sulphur, flowers of, as facial scrub, 34

Switzerland, ready-made clothing and, 60

tartar, removal of, 37

tea: beef, 8; at high altitudes, 62; and self-consciousness, 38; and servicemen, 81

teeth, knives held between, 96; *see also* toothache

tents, effeminacy of, 59; Napoleonic disdain for, 59

thumbs, and economical use of string, 96

tigers, fear of human gaze, 71

timepieces, public consultation of a sign of ill-breeding, 19

toads, powdered, 3

tobacco: beneficial effects of smoking upon the health, 88; diuretic powers of, 6; eye-watering inhalation of, 64; imaginative adaptation of instruments for smoking, 63–4; and moderation in children, 51; promotion of male bonding through, 88–9; as stimulus to the rectum, 6; superiority of pipe-smoking, 89; welcome after hunting giraffe, 87

tongue: perceptible assistance of in freeing teeth from food, 23; baked elephant trunk's resemblance to, 25; and roast udders, 27

toothache: curative properties of cats and, 1; haddock jaw-bones as remedy for, 1; and power of prayer, 1; relief from provided by chewing tobacco, 6

tread, elastic, 19

turtles: culinary preparation of, 26; inferior to boiled hippopotamus skin, 29

Tyrol region, and alcoholic guides, 62

udders, well boiled, 27

Velasquez, Diego, artistry of comparable to capital punishment, 91

ventriloquism, secret art of, 100–2

views, mountain-top, healthy influence of, 63

vinegar: aversion of gnats to, 1; dainty perfume of as body rub, 33; hippopotamus heads soused in, 29; and removal of freckles, 34

water: addiction to, 60; necessary ingredient for baptisms, 89

whooping cough, environmental remedies for, 11

womanhood, true, cheeks of crimsoned, 18

women, strange: significant smiles of, 41; houses of lead straight to death and hell, 42

working class, mobilisation of, 102–3

Workman, Dr William Hunter, long experience of alcohol, 62

writing, automatic, 68

Yakoma region, blood-brotherhood in, 58–9

youth, eternal, 32